FORUM FAVORITES

Volume 3

Al-Anon Family Group Headquarters, Inc.

New York • 1991

The Al-Anon Family Groups are a fellowship of relatives and friends of alcoholics who share their experience, strength and hope in order to solve their common problems. We believe alcoholism is a family illness and that changed attitudes can aid recovery.

Al-Anon is not allied with any sect, denomination, political entity, organization or institution; does not engage in any controversy, neither endorses nor opposes any cause. There are no dues for membership. Al-Anon is self-supporting through its own voluntary contributions.

Al-Anon has but one purpose: to help families of alcoholics. We do this by practicing the Twelve Steps, by welcoming and giving comfort to families of alcoholics, and by giving understanding and encouragement to the alcoholic.

The Suggested Preamble to the Twelve Steps

For Information and catalog of literature write:

**AL-ANON FAMILY GROUP HEADQUARTERS, INC.
P.O. BOX 862, MIDTOWN STATION
NEW YORK, NEW YORK 10018-0862
212-302-7240**

Library of Congress Catalog Card No. 91-72776
ISBN-910034-78-8
© AL-ANON FAMILY GROUP HEADQUARTERS, INC. 1991

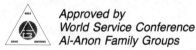

Approved by
World Service Conference
Al-Anon Family Groups

1-30M-91-5.00   B-9   PRINTED in U.S.A

Introduction

LOIS W., AL-ANON'S CO-FOUNDER, proposed publication of AL-ANON'S FAVORITE FORUM EDITORIALS at the 1970 World Service Conference. The first editor of *Al-Anon Family Group Forum,* Margaret D., was asked to choose her favorite editorials, and the book came into being that very year. The hardcover version was separated into two softcover books in 1982 titled, FORUM FAVORITES, Volumes 1 and 2, with the thought of someday publishing additional volumes.

In 1984 the Conference approved production of Volume 3 and the FORUM Editorial Committee set about the task of selection. This third volume of FORUM FAVORITES is a collection of FORUM editorials, or "inspirational articles" as Lois called them, published between 1974 and 1987.

Though similar in format to its predecessors, Volume 3 differs in that it includes articles from three different editors— Louise M.G., Hildegard M.V. and Fran H. The sharings present a personal and positive approach to the program and demonstrate the unique Al-Anon journey of each FORUM editor.

Contents

Introduction

Part III—Fran H.
Editor 1983-1987

Louise M. G.
Editor 1974–1977

"All of you have something very special to offer everyone else in Al-Anon: your experience and your self."

I Am Responsible For My Own Feelings

IT TOOK ME SUCH a long time to learn that I am responsible for the way I feel. I wanted to blame everyone for my unhappiness—my parents, my husband, life. If only I had been made to feel worthwhile as a child, I thought, I would now have a better self-image and wouldn't be so lacking in self-confidence, so fearful of rejection. If only I had married a non-alcoholic, I would be so much more carefree, so much more able to enjoy life. And life! Why did life have to be such a disappointment, such a hassle? Why couldn't nice things happen to me?

In Al-Anon, I was told I was responsible for my own happiness—the world didn't owe it to me; my husband didn't owe it to me; my parents didn't either. I had to stop feeling sorry for myself and start doing what would make me glad to be alive. For a long time, I had to make a daily effort to count my blessings. It helped to read the paper and see what was happening to other people. Newspapers seem to thrive on bad news. For a while, I could only count my blessings in reverse—at least this bad thing hadn't happened to me, or, I was better off than that poor soul.

The war in Vietnam was going on at the time, and the papers were full of pictures of refugees with their belongings on their backs, clothed in rags, half-starved. Looking at them, dispossessed, mutilated, knowing no comfort, it was easy to be grateful for my warm house with plumbing and clean sheets. At least I wasn't sleeping out in the rain on a rat and louse-infested straw pile. At least I was getting wholesome food and didn't know what it was to be really hungry. I could be grateful for living in a land without war, for having three healthy children. I began to be aware of my many blessings, and started to feel less sorry for myself.

Going to meetings helped, too, of course. There was always someone with a problem I could consider worse than mine.

As I began to be involved in my group, taking on various responsibilities, sponsoring newcomers, I came out of myself. The more aware I became of others, the smaller my problems seemed. As I did my job and saw that my efforts were helping others, my feelings of self-worth grew, and I began to be happy to be alive.

But I still had a problem with despair—a feeling of hopelessness, a deep, dark sadness that overwhelmed me at times and made me want to end it all. Eventually, I learned that my depressions were due to boiled-up anger. I had misunderstood the Al-Anon message not to argue with the alcoholic, and had stopped communicating altogether! Oh, we talked about non-controversial subjects, but I avoided telling him how I felt about anything. Not only did I not express my anger; I *felt* guilty about having it in the first place! I thought if I were practicing my program, if I fully accepted him as sick, nothing he did could make me angry. I didn't realize anger was a normal response to a frustrating situation and that I had a right to my feelings. What I did about them was something else. But I did owe it to myself to find a healthy outlet for my anger. Bottling it up until I lost control or became so depressed I wanted to die was not the answer.

I began to talk to my husband again—to let him know how his behavior made me feel. He did, after all, have a right to know how he was affecting those around him. I couldn't expect him to act differently if he was unaware of the effects of his actions on me. Even after he did become aware, he often chose to continue acting the same way. That was his choice. I couldn't change him—but I had changed what I could—I had let my feelings out.

Other times, he would get very sad and upset when I told him how I felt. Not wanting to hurt him, I was tempted to keep things to myself. But again, I had to learn and relearn that, just as I couldn't blame him for my unhappiness, I couldn't allow him to blame me for his. Making me feel guilty for hurting his feelings was just another way he had to control me, but only if I allowed it.

I don't always like to hear what other people have to say, but I don't have to let it hurt or depress me. I take it for what it's worth and move on from there. If it's a worthwhile criticism, I'm thankful for the insight and make the necessary changes. If it's not worthwhile or accurate, I simply dismiss it. On the other hand, I don't deliberately say or do anything to hurt someone else. I try always to be tactful and kind, but honest.

I have stopped feeling so responsible for the feelings of others. My own feelings are a big enough responsibility.

Unless You Become as Little Children

I WAS REMINDED of this quotation from the New Testament the other evening as I was listening to a concert in the park and watching a small child listen to it in his way. "Unless you become as little children," I thought, "you'll miss so much of the joy of living that you won't recognize heaven when you get there!"

The musical selections were all happy, lilting, gay and even exuberant, in keeping with the carefree spirit of summer. It was a celebration of life and joy and I thought how true it is that music is the universal language, the language of the soul. I felt closer to the musicians and composers and the other people in the audience than I do to some people I know who talk on and on, without ever communicating their feelings!

Over to the side of the stage, there stood this little boy, no more than 6 or 7, who was watching the conductor in a very intent, serious way. All of a sudden he started to smile, and move his arms in imitation. Like magic, almost as if the music had taken possession of him and filled every cell of his body, he began to dance. He twirled and swirled, his movements seeming to anticipate the rhythms and changes in the music. He was absolutely delightful and delighted. What a beautiful way to be, I thought!

Just then, his stern father interrupted him and told him to sit down and be quiet, although he wasn't near anyone, or obstructing anyone's view. The child was obedient, and saddened, and while he continued to keep time with the music by kicking the dirt, it was obvious he wasn't having nearly as much fun.

How like that father we are to ourselves, I thought. We impose restrictions on ourselves, mistakenly trying to impress others or live up to their expectations of us, and we rob ourselves of the freedom to enjoy what is beautiful. We crowd our lives with musts and shoulds and can'ts and oughts, and become so bogged down with work, routine and problems that we're not even conscious of the great beauty that surrounds us.

On my way to work, I travel along a road whose shoulders are covered with weeds—but even these burst into bloom. Queen Anne's lace, wild black-eyed Susans, day lilies and little blue flowers whose name I don't know cover the ground. I remember, as a child, bringing home bouquets of wildflowers to my mother, clutched tightly in my hot little fists, so that the stems were practically cooked! But I was so excited about finding these beautiful blossoms that I didn't want to lose a single one by holding them too loosely. Now the neighbors' children and my own do the same for me.

As children, we all had the capacity for unlimited joy of living and appreciating beauty. Perhaps it was the short distance from our eyes to the ground that made it so. Let's not allow our greater stature to steal our ability to rejoice and feel good all over!

Lust for Life—A Precious Gift

HERE IN AMERICA, our thoughts traditionally turn to counting our blessings as our national holiday of Thanksgiving approaches. I find it easy now to appreciate the abundance that surrounds me as I drive in the country and see piles of golden pumpkins, and observe the rich harvest of apples, grapes and corn. I can get high on just the fragrance of cider, drying leaves and hay.

The crisp days of autumn and the dazzling brilliance of the landscape fill me with wonder at the infinite variety and the endless flow of life from one form into another.

These things have always been here. And yet, it wasn't so long ago that I could see nothing to be happy about. What did it matter, all this abundance, when I was so unhappy? I was jealous of those who had more than I, who seemed well-adjusted and full of life. I wished every day that I would die and be released from my grim prison.

Not knowing how to cope with alcoholism, having failed at my self-appointed mission—getting my husband sober—and resenting my lot in life, I believed myself to be the unlucky victim of fate, without hope of ever escaping. In a desperate effort to find relief, I resorted to the death of my feelings. I wasn't aware of what I was doing, of course. I became a robot, going through the motions of living, but feeling nothing. I never cried nor laughed, got upset, nor enjoyed. It was as though I'd been locked out, condemned to observing life through a pane of glass.

Al-Anon taught me life didn't have to be all pain or all numbness. I could look at the positive, count my blessings, find answers to my problems—in short, make my own happiness. When I no longer found it necessary to run from reality, I began to feel again.

It was a long time before I could feel deeply. I gained courage as I dared to trust others with the truth about myself;

to risk being hurt in order to experience happiness; as I let go of my unrealistic goals; as I took a chance I'd be disappointed in order to make a commitment, believe in someone.

It was worth the price. Today I feel vibrant with life, fully potent and eager to experience whatever is in store for me. I'm open to the full gamut of feelings. Life had become a challenge, a joy, a privilege, even a pain at times. Of all the blessings I have received in Al-Anon, this is my most cherished—my lust for life.

Merry Christmas

ARE YOU APPROACHING the holiday season with a heavy heart? Are you facing your first or another Christmas alone? Is the alcoholic you love still drinking, evoking fears of past Christmases ruined? Are you finding it difficult to relax as the holidays approach because you're afraid the alcoholic may slip? Are you feeling depressed because you can't afford to have the kind of celebration you'd like? Are you feeling sorry for yourself because you don't have the time you'd like to shop and prepare and decorate?

Think how lucky you are! No matter what your problem, Al-Anon can make it lighter. For instance, no one in Al-Anon need ever be alone; a little thinking ahead of time can bring together those of us who will be alone, to share in mutual joy and warmth. Years ago, when I was looking forward to the possibility of having to leave my home right before Christmas, an Al-Anon friend responded with, "If you have to leave, just come to us. We'll find room for you," "With the children?" "With the children." I never had to take her up on it, but the comfort of knowing I had a place to go, a person who cared, carried me through many difficult hours.

Another Christmas that comes to mind is one when our meeting night fell on Christmas Eve. We'd decided to have a meeting, just in case someone needed it, and two members volunteered to go down and open the building. About 7:00 that evening, I received a Twelfth Step call from a very troubled girl whose husband was in jail. She was pregnant, totally distraught, without transportation. Luckily, my preparations for the holiday were all made, and I was able to get her and take her to a meeting that night. The look in her eyes was the best gift I received that year.

I have a dear friend who carries the spirit of Christmas with her every day of the year. She is always giving of herself, her time, her affection, understanding and love. She loves to give presents—not because she needs to be loved and is trying to make others like her, but because she has so much to give that she receives genuine pleasure and delight from such giving. Her joy is doubled when she sees the joy she has occasioned in another.

On her birthday, the only wish I could think of making for her was that she receive what she gives every day.

I wish for you that, whatever your problems this year, you may find the comfort and solace I have found in Al-Anon, and that you may all someday be like my friend—fully loving and happy human beings.

Discussion of The First Step

We admitted we were powerless over alcohol—that our lives had became unmanageable.

Although I never felt responsible for my husband's drinking problem, I did feel responsible for finding the answer. He drank too much when I met him, and I knew the drinking would be a major problem after we were married, but I didn't know it was alcoholism.

I thought he drank because he was unhappy, spoiled and immature, and that our marriage would change all that. The responsibilities of husband and father would make him grow up, and I would be able to change the things that made him unhappy. I would love him into changing. Someone has aptly described that approach to a relationship as the "frog prince myth."

Setting out in my own immature way with these unrealistic goals, I was a ridiculous combination of Joan of Arc and the fairy princess. Concentrating on solving someone else's problems and changing someone else's character became my way of life. It was terribly frustrating, but then I have a lot of perseverance and fortitude, (that's polite for stubborn), and so the battle raged on. My life was becoming unmanageable, not only because I was trying to manage something that couldn't be managed— my husband's drinking and behavior, but also because I wasn't spending much time managing what could be managed—myself.

I have since learned that we act according to the way we feel, not necessarily according to what makes sense. We satisfy our emotional needs, whether or not we are aware of them.

My attempt to try to control my husband's drinking in spite of one failure after another was fulfilling my need to be needed. After all, I rationalized, my husband would never be able to make it without me. It was fulfilling my need to feel important— how easy it is to look important when assuming all responsibilities and pointing out the failures of others. It was fulfilling my need for admiration—how I loved it when people said I must be an angel to put up with his antics. And it was fulfilling my need to deceive myself—I was scared silly to look at myself.

Like the alcoholic, I had to hit bottom. The painful consequences of my behavior finally outweighed the emotional "benefits" I was receiving from this relationship. I asked for help. When I came into Al-Anon, I had completely surrendered, completely given up, completely admitted failure.

Admitting I was powerless over my husband's drinking wasn't hard—experience had proven that to me a hundred thousand times over. And realizing I wasn't responsible for the answer was a terrific relief. I could also easily admit my life was unmanageable, with my crippling depressions, uncontrollable rages and endless fantasies.

However, I discovered that a change in knowledge doesn't necessarily mean a change in behavior. I should have known it already—my husband had admitted he was an alcoholic, and yet he continued to drink! I admitted I was powerless, yet for a long time I continued to be obsessed with his behavior, to base my decisions on how they would affect him, to try new approaches to motivate him to stop drinking. Although my knowledge had changed, my behavior hadn't.

Looking at my behavior helped me to understand these needs I wasn't aware of, and gradually I changed. At first, Al-Anon filled my needs to be needed, to feel important, to be admired. After a while, I was able to let go of the need to deceive myself. Eventually, what I had learned did sink in to a feeling level, and I finally felt comfortable in my heart about doing what my head knew was right.

Discussion of The Second Step

Came to believe that a Power greater than ourselves could restore us to sanity.

Certainly, by the time I arrived at Al-Anon, I could no longer consider myself sane. My days were spent in fear—my husband didn't have the shakes, but I did. I was afraid of what people thought, afraid of what my husband might do, afraid of what would become of us and our three children, afraid even to talk on the telephone; I was afraid the words wouldn't come out right. At night, I slept in a taut, rolled-up ball, and wondered why all my muscles ached during the day.

I vacillated between wishing my husband would die a horrible death and praying he'd make it safely home.

Although I still cared about appearances and tried hard to keep up a good front, I began to neglect myself at home. When I did go out, I took great pains to appear perfect, but raced home, afraid to talk to people. As I felt more and more trapped, I resorted to the comfort of fantasies. Eventually, these fantasies absorbed most of my waking hours, and I became like a zombie—performing my household duties in a mechanical fashion, my mind far away. If my children interrupted my reveries to demand attention, I became annoyed.

I was totally obsessed with my husband's drinking and spent all of my time with him nagging him, arguing bitterly, trying so hard to make him see what he was doing to himself and to me. Although I knew it was useless, I did it anyway, because I didn't know what else to do. Surely, there must be a solution, I thought, and vaguely hoped to stumble upon it while applying home remedies.

When I came into Al-Anon, I readily admitted my power-lessness over alcohol and the fact that my life had become unmanageable. As I looked around the meeting room at the serene faces of others who were living with alcoholism, it became immediately apparent that they had found the answers I had been so desperately groping for four and a half years. I could believe in the power of Al-Anon, if nothing else.

Over the years, my understanding of my Higher Power has changed many times. But in the beginning, it sufficed for me to believe in the power of the program and the group. I was totally ready to do what they told me, without question. And the results, of course, were nothing short of miraculous.

Discussion of the Third Step

Made a decision to turn our will and our lives over to the care of God as we understood Him.
It wasn't until I'd taken the Fourth Step that I was able to take the Third. Having had this long-standing need to appear perfect, it had been a long time since I'd really looked at myself. It was so much more comfortable to concentrate on the faults of others! However, with the love of the group, and the courage I received from listening to others share, I was able, finally, to admit I was emotionally ill, and had been for a long time—long before I'd met my husband. And then, the awful admission to myself that I didn't know how to love, and was, in fact, incapable of it because I didn't love myself.

My sense of values were so distorted that I equated love with suffering and concluded I must love my husband an awful lot because I sure was suffering! But once I'd honestly admitted I didn't love my husband, and never had, I was seized with a terrible anxiety—"How can I continue to live with a man I don't love? I certainly can't live a lie, and yet, I don't feel I can make it on my own. How can my children learn to love if their parents don't know how?"

I suddenly felt an overwhelming need to pray and turned to my Higher Power, the God of my understanding, whom I then saw as a powerful, loving being, ready and willing to help me. I prayed for help, to learn how to love.

It wasn't long afterward that I began to gain all sorts of new insights. There were meetings and talks on love, books on love, things that probably had always been around, but I was seeing them for the first time. And, of course, as I was accepted and loved by the group, I began to accept and love myself, and to find in me the capacity to love others. Eventually, I was able to love my husband in spite of his drinking and to want him to get well, not just for my sake, but for his. I became able to do what was good for him, not necessarily what he wanted me to do, and saw in him many fine qualities I'd overlooked.

That was many years ago, and just the beginning. This Step took me much further. All the Steps are important, and we couldn't do without any one of them. But this Step is central, I think, and essential to my serenity. It is this Step that gives me the courage to make decisions because I firmly believe that, as long as I'm doing my best, things will work out for the best, even if it's not the way I want them to work out. It is this Step that gives me fortitude because I know that any problems or difficulties confronting me today are really opportunities for growth which I can use to become a better person. It is this Step which saves me from worry because I know God's will is being done for me, and that can only be for my good, even if it doesn't feel good right now.

As long as I'm doing my best, I don't have to worry about results. They are God's province. I look at all the things over which I have no control as God's will for me today, and accept them as they come. I allow my life to happen, instead of trying to control everything about it. I believe there is a force for good—a master plan, if you will—and that I can either work with it, in harmony, or try to swim upstream, exhausting myself and not getting anywhere. This Step is not a masochistic relinquishment of my right to be the director of my own life. Rather, it sets me free to *be* myself, in charge of my life and my decisions because I can act without fear and accept without question.

Discussion of the Fourth Step

Made a searching and fearless moral inventory of ourselves.
    A recent meeting on the "checklist for evaluating maturity" *(Alcoholism the Family Disease)* reminded me of the first

attempt I made at the Fourth Step. I'd used that checklist to guide myself in my very first inventory-taking, and couldn't find one positive thing! Not being able to see any good in myself was one of my problems then—that is, when I wasn't kidding myself that I was perfect. I couldn't find the happy medium.

I'd been premature in taking the Fourth Step, but felt such a need to do it at the time that I couldn't move ahead without it. Although I benefitted from that early inventory and came to grips with some very real shortcomings, it took some time before I could be more objective about myself. I do think it's important to wait a while before taking Step Four. As has been said in our literature, first we must detach from the alcoholic problem. We can't take an honest inventory if we're still blaming others for our problems. Then, we must accept ourselves if the prospect of looking at ourselves is to be anything short of terrifying. And we usually come by this self-acceptance via the love of the group. It takes some people longer to feel comfortable than others. And finally, our thinking should be clear so that we can make accurate appraisals of ourselves.

Just as I had difficulty seeing myself as a person who was neither all good nor all bad, I had difficulty determining the effects of my actions on others. Like a child who imagines he's really knocked an adult over with a feather when the adult pretends to be thrown off balance, I imagined myself to be much more powerful than I was in my relationships with others.

Convinced my parents' happiness depended on me, I carried a lot of guilt for having let them down by making an unhappy marriage. I thought I'd broken their hearts. The truth was that they were hurt to see my pain, but their happiness was derived from many sources, not just me.

Having had countless bitter arguments with my husband's mother, I imagined I was responsible for all her emotional problems. The truth was, she simply turned me off and discounted what I said. She'd had problems long before meeting me!

It was only with time and the help of others that I was finally able to realistically and accurately evaluate the extent of the damage I'd done to others.

While searching for my shortcomings, I fell into a different kind of trap. I identified some shortcomings as good qualities, and some of these as shortcomings. For instance, I thought I was very patient and tolerant because I never got angry if people kept me waiting, cut in front of me on a line, took the parking spot I was waiting for. The fact was, I had such a poor self-image, it never occurred to me I had a right to assert myself, and I was terrified of conflict. I was a doormat in every area of my life. It was a big mistake to see that as a virtue.

On the other hand, I identified anger as one of my greatest shortcomings, not realizing that anger is a feeling and, as such, is neither good nor bad. It's how we express it that makes the difference between a mature person and one who is immature, between a constructive attitude and one that is destructive. It was a long while before I was able to feel angry without feeling guilty, and then to express my anger in appropriate ways.

One of the greatest helps I had in taking my inventory was a friend who saw me objectively. When I'd discuss certain aspects of my inventory with her, she'd listen and then let me know when she thought I was off base. By holding up the mirror of reality—not allowing me to see myself as better or worse than I was—she helped me to focus on the areas that really needed attention. This is, to my mind, one of the most valuable helps we can get from a good sponsor.

Discussion of the Fifth Step

Admitted to God, to ourselves and to another human being the exact nature of our wrongs.

What wonderful relief I felt when I took this Step! Admitting my faults, mistakes and wrong actions to myself was hard. But that was taken care of in the Fourth Step. Admitting them to God was easy because I never doubted His acceptance of me and forgiveness, if I wanted it. And I did.

Admitting my wrongs to another human being, however, was something else again. But I'd been so miserable before Al-Anon, and had experienced such a dramatic change in my life since trying to apply the program, that I never doubted its wisdom. I knew this admission was necessary. And, having had an honest look at myself and what I'd done, I really needed to unload.

Selection of the proper person is important, I think. I chose someone whose opinion I respected and whose discretion I trusted—my clergyman. He was patient, kind and understanding as I went on and on. A miracle of recovery took place in that room. I went in feeling unlovable, unacceptable and guilty. As I shared my innermost secrets with him and he continued to accept me, I began to see myself as not so horrible after all—only human.

Once I'd shared myself in this way with another human being and had been fully accepted as I was, I was able to accept myself, and to continue to share myself with others. Eventually, there was nothing about me that the group didn't know. I had said in effect, "Here I am—this is the real me—without any phoniness, without any facades, without any masks." The more I shared, the more I was loved! No one has ever rejected me for what I am and have done and, much to my surprise at first, many people identified with me.

Once my clergyman accepted me, I began to accept myself. Then my group loved me, and I began to love myself. Thus began a process of growth that continues, via the Tenth Step, to this day.

Ten years later, as I look back on that original inventory and sharing, I can see how limited my vision was. But it was as honest as it could be at that time, and that's important. I needed to be accepted as I thought I was. Once shared, my picture of myself was altered as my awareness changed and as I changed.

Nothing can replace the comfort and security of knowing we are loved and accepted just the way we are.

Discussion of the Sixth Step

Were entirely ready to have God remove all these defects of character.

One thing becomes clearer and clearer with time. I must be constantly vigilant, and work this program continuously. Otherwise, the gains I have made quickly fade away and I revert to the way I was before I came to Al-Anon.

I had no difficulty admitting I was powerless over alcohol, but found myself trying to control my husband's sobriety. Time and time again I caught myself focusing on, "If I do this, maybe it will help *him* to see what *he's* doing."

The same thing applies to letting go and deciding to let God direct my life. I realized that was a sensible approach and was totally sincere when I took Step Three. But unless I watch myself, I find I'm trying to run things again, to be in control.

By the time I got to Step Six, I thought I was ready to give up all my defects. I certainly didn't like what I'd seen in Step Four. But I didn't realize how much I enjoyed my self-right-eousness, smugness, and feelings of superiority. I wasn't aware of how much I got out of being in control, directing things.

Without thinking twice, *I* decided to work on *my* character, forgetting that this Step says *God* is the one who is going to do the removing. I went hard to work on myself, and got nowhere.

Finally, I had to go back to the Third Step and turn my life and my will over to my Higher Power all over again. To me, Step Six is the key to relaxing in this program. We don't have to push and shove and exact a frantic pace from ourselves in order to improve overnight. This Step tells us God will take care of it, and we assume, in His own good time.

When I let go, Step Six began to work for me. I realized that my Higher Power would help me by allowing me to encounter opportunities to grow and to strengthen my character, would give me insight to recognize these opportunities for what they were, and would provide the strength to deal with them. All I had to do was keep an open mind and be willing to change as the need became apparent.

Discussion of the Seventh Step

Humbly asked Him to remove our shortcomings.

My Higher Power is Love. To me, love is the greatest healing force, the source of all life and renewal. It is expressed in many ways in my life, but especially through people—the members of my group, my friends, my family.

It was the love of the group that helped me to face myself and which has supported me while I have grown. Powered by this love, I can face life without fear.

To me, humbly asking God to remove my shortcomings means realizing that I cannot afford to shut myself off from people. I must go to them with my fears, doubts, pain, guilt and anxieties. I must not run from them because I fear losing their love. It is the act of running away, the refusal to share myself, that makes me feel unloved. Humbly asking God to

remove my shortcomings means asking people to help me.
As with most things, I've learned this the hard way. One
would think that, after having had the wonderful experience
of once being totally accepted by the group, I would never
again doubt that acceptance, and could always be comfortable
being myself. Not so.

Every once in a while, I forget. I fall into the trap of fearing
rejection, usually because I haven't lived up to my own unrealistic expectations and I'm unhappy with myself. For example, after several years in the program, I began to think I
had to live up to an image—my own fantasy of what I thought
an old-timer in the program ought to be. I mentally rewrote
the Twelfth Step to say, *"successfully* practicing these principles
in all our affairs."* I began to think of myself only in terms
of the helper, forgetting that we never stop needing help.
When I failed, I was ashamed to share my failure with the
group, afraid they'd reject me for not living up to their expectations. In short, I'd lost my humility—my ability to accept
myself.

Actually, I was projecting my own expectations of myself
onto them. They were much more realistic and I must say
much kinder in their expectations of me than I was. They
allowed me to make mistakes.

My standard way of reacting to alcoholism and to all the
other things in my life that had frightened or upset me—to
run and hide, to withdraw from people, was in full swing
again. I'd cut myself off from love, from God, from the very
thing that could make me well. The more I ran away and tried
to hide my problems from others, the more fearful I became,
the more convinced that I was unlovable.

Luckily, my friends soon saw what was wrong and helped
me get back on the right track. I hope I never again react to
my anger at myself by cutting myself off from those who love
me. That only doubles the anguish, and is the very block that
prevents me from overcoming my shortcomings.

Discussion of Step Eight

Made a list of all persons we had harmed, and became willing to make amends to them all.

One of my problems has always been that I take on guilt that really isn't mine. When I made my list of those I'd harmed, it was loaded with things that were not my fault. I had to talk to members of the group who could tell me when I was assuming responsibility for things that weren't my doing. I hadn't yet learned to be as tolerant of myself as I was of others. That began with Step Nine, when I made amends to myself.

I eventually made up an accurate list of those I had harmed. To be sure, I had harmed my husband—not purposely, of course—but I had nevertheless done him real harm through my ignorance of alcoholism, my self-righteousness, my lack of self-respect and self-esteem, my inability to love in a responsible way. I had no doubt enabled him to drink by covering up for him and by removing the painful consequences of his behavior. I had added to his burden of guilt by blaming him for my self-imposed martyrdom. I had eroded his self-esteem with my cutting sarcasm. I had encouraged the very dependency I resented by behaving more like a mother than a wife. I had, in anger, punished him, derided him, and stomped all over his feelings. I had let him know and feel how inadequate I thought he was. Even the hardiest cactus would have found it impossible to grow in that hostile environment!

True, I'd been incapable of mature love because I didn't love myself. But the fact that I couldn't do otherwise at the time and wasn't deliberately destructive didn't make my behavior any less damaging. The end result was the same, and I certainly wanted to make amends once I saw what I had done and felt so terribly, terribly sorry.

The children, too, had been scarred and damaged by my behavior. Torn apart with my own emotional problems, I'd been unable to provide them with a consistent, firm, loving environment. They were forced constantly to test the limits I set for them because they never knew when those limits would be enforced. They had been the victims of my displaced rage; had been deprived of a good model for adult behavior; had not had adequate supervision or response to their emotional needs. At times, as I tried to imagine what it must be like to perceive the world through their young eyes, to see what they saw and feel how they felt, I would become overwhelmed with guilt and the awful conviction that I'd been a failure as a mother. Again, my friends in the group would remind we that no one is perfect, that we all make mistakes, that the guilt would ease as I began to make amends.

Finally, I placed myself on the list, realizing I'd harmed myself by accepting the unacceptable and by putting all my energies to work on something that couldn't be changed— my husband's alcoholism. I'd shortchanged myself and turned my life into a nightmare where all I knew was failure, despair, isolation, terror and rage. I'd denied myself the richness of life, the warmth of friendship, the comfort of honesty, the satisfaction of accomplishment. By constantly beating myself down for what I wasn't doing instead of rejoicing in what I was doing well, I'd shut off every avenue of positive feeling and healthy growth.

I could hardly wait to move to Step Nine and begin to set things right.

Discussion of Step Nine

Made direct amends to such people wherever possible, except when to do so would injure them or others.

In many ways, this is my favorite Step. It made me feel so good, and I like to feel good. Each time I did something to even the score and make up for some of the harm I'd done, the burden of guilt became lighter. One of the rocks in the bag I was carrying had been taken out and used to rebuild relationships.

I made amends to my husband by loving him in a responsible way, recognizing his qualities and being openly appreciative of his efforts to please me. Courtesy, praise, warmth, compassion and acceptance became my goals. His favorite dishes became a must on my menu. I even learned to cook Long Island duckling!

Instead of telling him what to do and how to do it, I practiced letting him do what he wanted to do in his own way. When he got into trouble as the result of his drinking or irresponsible behavior, I kept my hands off. Also, I realized that allowing him to bully me into doing something I didn't want to do, would only be destructive. So I learned to stand firm and refuse to be manipulated. And I learned to say "I'm sorry," no matter what the reaction.

Where the children were concerned, I had to start by learning to be a firm, loving, consistent parent. What they needed most at first was a mother who set limits on their behavior and always enforced them in the same way. I tried to be fair, to listen to their feelings, to respect their opinions, to avoid arbitrary decisions. But I also knew that, until they developed internal controls, I would have to give them the security they needed by providing the controls for them. Threats became a thing of the past. I learned to praise and criticize what they did instead of judging them. I read books and tried to apply principles of sound mental health to my relationship with them.

To make up for the emotional deprivation they'd suffered, I decided to give each child a day a month of undivided attention. I'd hire a sitter for the other two, and would plan a day of special activities around each child's interests. What lovely days we had, and what wonders came about as a result!

Where others were concerned, I tried to be the kind of person I'd like to be with if I were in the other's shoes. To my mother-in-law, I became the kind of daughter-in-law I'd like to have.

Someone once said, "If you can't make amends to the person you've harmed, do good to someone else instead." How easy to be helpful, agreeable and kind to strangers with this in mind! And what a nice feeling to know that guilt doesn't have to be carried forever because the person who was hurt is no longer around.

Part of my amends to myself included getting professional help to correct the deep emotional problems that were preventing me from being as happy and as fully alive as I wanted to be. I went back to school, met new people, spread my wings. I'd done myself harm by being a silent martyr, so I learned to recognize, accept and express my feelings, and to start being good to myself. I bought new clothes, went to the doctor and dentist, found friends with whom I could do the things I liked to do.

Instead of accepting unacceptable behavior, I decided what I wanted from life and how I wanted to live. I refused to compromise my integrity—to make concessions on important issues merely to appease.

Making amends has helped me to become a person I can like and love.

Discussion of Step Ten

Continued to take personal inventory and when we were wrong promptly admitted it.

This Step reminds me that learning to live is an ongoing process; that I will never be finished. The people who wrote the Steps expected me to fail, to be wrong, to make mistakes.

Why then is it so hard for me to admit it when it happens?

The lesson I learned long ago is deeply ingrained: "Perfection is the price you must pay for love." Although I now know it's not true, and that I have gotten myself into trouble whenever I have acted as if it were, it is still a part of me and comes back to haunt me if I allow myself to become complacent.

I have been blessed with the ability to do many things well. It is a gift, and I don't take credit for the talent, although I do feel responsible for making good use of my abilities. But what happens to me is that people often tend to put me on a pedestal and expect perfection.

When I was all caught up in my need for approval, trying to live up to the unrealistic expectations of others became a terrible burden. I found myself doing everything to please others and nothing for myself. The need to be perfect spread to my Al-Anon program and I became uncomfortable telling it the way it was at meetings for fear of disillusioning newcomers. Admitting what I'd done before Al-Anon was easy: everybody was doing it, it was ancient history, and I had an excuse—that was *before* the program! But admitting what I was doing after years of program—that was something else. What a line I'd fed myself!

I didn't become comfortable with admitting mistakes in the here and now until I'd fully accepted myself as lovable in spite of my faults. It isn't easy to say "I'm sorry," but it feels so much better than pretending I'm right when I know I'm not.

My children know I'm interested in their welfare and that I like to be fair. And so some of my decisions are subjected to arbitration; we respect each other's intelligence, and they know I will change my mind if I see I was wrong in my thinking. It makes for stimulating conversations and keeps me on my toes; there's no totalitarianism in our house, but a lot of respect and appreciation for each other.

With Step Ten, the dictum which applies is not, "Haste

Makes Waste," but "He Who Hesitates Is Lost." The sooner
I admit my mistake and apologize or put it right, the better.
Even if I have to face a distasteful "I told you so," or "If
you'd listened to me," I feel better for having said I made a
mistake. The longer I put it off, the harder it becomes.
The first nine Steps help us to recover. The last three help
to keep us well and getting better. Step Ten insures a strong
moral fiber and makes us easier to live with.

Discussion of Step Eleven

*Sought through prayer and meditation to improve our conscious
contact with God as we understood Him, praying only for
knowledge of His will for us, and the power to carry that out.*

All of us, I suppose, have our own concept of God, and it
is this very freedom of belief which makes our program so
attractive. During my years in Al-Anon, my spiritual beliefs
have undergone tremendous change. There have been times
when I felt impelled to study and meditate and learn a great
deal in order to sort out my thoughts, attitudes and relationship
to God. At other times it sufficed to take merely a reflective
moment or so during the day to reevaluate the direction my
life was taking. There was also a period of great spiritual pain,
when my old beliefs no longer gave me comfort or solace, but
I hadn't yet found other answers—sort of like a journey through
a long, dark tunnel. My childish faith had been an important
part of my identity, and when it became meaningless to me,
I felt like an amputee, very much as though my person had
been mutilated and disfigured. It hurt for a long time until I
could find new answers, give my Higher Power a new identity,
feel comfortable with my new faith. Sometimes I had to put
aside my search and take time to integrate and assimilate the
new ideas, thoughts and beliefs. Gradually, I came to a new

understanding of my Higher Power which continues to grow and evolve as I do the same.

Today, I find it especially necessary to meditate and collect my spirit when going through times of emotional stress and turmoil. Early morning is my favorite time. During this past year's difficult months, I would rise a half hour early, and while the rest of the house was quiet, would play some classical music, or some of my records made to encourage meditation— the sounds of temple bells, or birds, the ocean. And with this quiet, peaceful background, I would sit and slowly look at some of the beautiful nature photographs in my special books, or read a few passages from some inspirational literature. It was like taking a trip to a quiet retreat, at one with nature and the universe. I would let my thoughts flow as I gazed at pictures of leaves or sunsets or snow, or as my mind caught a particularly helpful idea, and would try to sense a feeling of harmony with God, the force for good that flows through the universe.

Prayerful reflection on my plans, actions and decisions and daily reexamination of my motives helped me to remain strong and serene in the face of many upsetting and destructive situations.

Years ago, I used to recite prayers written by others which I had memorized as a child. The only prayers I said were prayers of supplication (asking) and prayers of thanks. It didn't occur to me then, that trying to understand my relationship to the universal whole, trying to figure out my purpose in life, trying to fulfill my potential by doing my best—these are prayers, too.

Today I don't pray for things any more. I know that the events and people which enter my life can all enrich me if I am filled with love and make a constant effort to become better.

Discussion of Step Twelve

Having had a spiritual awakening as the result of these Steps, we tried to carry this message to others, and to practice these principles in all our affairs.

My spirit was so beaten down, defeated and hopeless before I found this beautiful fellowship of love. I believed life was a burden, a punishment imposed on me for some vague crime committed long ago by people I didn't know. I didn't like myself, felt I was unworthy of love, and didn't believe I had the ability to do anything about my problems. Pain and despair were constant.

Through the practice of the Steps, I gradually became a completely different person. My spirit awakened to the joy and beauty of life lived in love—love of myself, love of others. As I made decisions and changed the things I could, I became more self-confident until finally I arrived at the point where I believe that, with the help of my Higher Power, I can face any life situation. I feel comfortable, adequate and deserving of life's bounty.

Life now is an exciting challenge, a joyous celebration. My acceptance of myself as I am and of others as they are has taken away my driven, anxious need to impress others and control everyone. There's just a nice, warm glow inside.

It was not long after I came into Al-Anon that I began to go out speaking. I'd found a gold-mine, and I wanted to shout to the world that here was an answer to all those perplexing mysteries surrounding alcoholism; here was an answer to fear and loneliness and pain; here was an answer to life.

What I found, as most of you have, is that by helping others, we help ourselves; by spreading the message, we keep it and it grows. The Serenity Prayer and the Prayer of Saint Francis hang on the wall above my bed. These two are my goals; daily reminders of what I want to be. It truly is "in giving that we receive."

I try to make the Al-Anon philosophy pervade all I do. It has become so much a part of me that I could no more separate it from myself than I could lose my personality. The wisdom of this program is so profound, we can never plumb its depths. It applies to everything we do, from rearing children to cleaning house to playing to mourning. It is a constant source of sustenance.

Self-Love Overcomes Need to Suffer

THE IMAGE OF THE selfless, self-effacing martyr who gives up everything for the love of others had always appealed to me. Somehow, when I sacrificed for others, I felt so superior and so righteous. Actually, we often go out of our way to please those we love, and willingly make sacrifices for them: parents give up their sleep to watch over a sick child; they forego vacations and new clothes to provide education for their youngsters; a wife will give up an evening with friends to attend a company function with her husband; a husband will spend an afternoon installing curtain rods instead of reading the paper and listening to music.

When we love, we want to do these things because it pleases us. We are enriched by the very doing and need no other reward.

But I chose self-sacrifice for far different reasons. I thought being a martyr would make me admirable in the eyes of others; would gain me approval, even glory. I thought others would be so grateful to me, they would give me their undying love. Believing I was essentially worthless, I chose martyrdom as the path to gaining worth. I married an active alcoholic, aware that our lives would be a series of problems, because I wanted the glory and recognition I thought would be forthcoming when I straightened him out, even at the expense of my own happiness.

However, no one wanted to play the script as I had written it. My husband continued to drink, no matter how many sacrifices I made, no matter how much I gave up for him. Instead of being grateful to me, he was angry and resentful. And where I had expected admiration and approval, I received pity and rejection. I cried because my husband had no respect for me, paid no attention to my needs, belittled my accomplishments, ridiculed me. My life was one of confused agony. I was paying the price—where was my reward?

It was in Al-Anon that I learned my kind of self-inflicted suffering was not admirable; it was sick. It was here, too, I learned that if I longed for the respect of others, I had to start by respecting myself. Al-Anon corrected my mistaken conviction that I was worthless and told me every human being is worthwhile in and of himself.

Establishing justice in my home; not suffering the painful consequences of someone else's behavior; doing what was best for me; treating myself like an important person; refusing to tolerate unacceptable behavior—these were all new ideas to me, and it took time before I could apply them consistently. The image of the sainted martyr died hard.

First, I had to get to know myself, my qualities, strengths, abilities, faults, needs, the things that gave me pleasure. This took time and is still going on. But I couldn't begin to love myself until I found out who I was.

Next, I had to care enough about myself to be good to myself: get the proper medical attention, take time to rest, leave time for play as well as work, allow myself some luxuries. This took much effort and made me feel incredibly guilty at first. But now it's become a good habit.

Self-respect followed as I insisted on my freedom as a human being to select my values, choose my career, fulfill myself as a person. I met with a great deal of resistance and opposition from people who didn't want me to change. Only the knowledge that my integrity and eventual happiness were at stake kept me from giving in to the unreasonable demands of others who wanted to possess me, control me, show me off, live vicariously through me.

Finally, I had to assume the responsibility for my welfare, choosing not necessarily what I felt like doing, but what I knew would give me the greatest benefit in terms of emotional and spiritual growth.

As I continue to practice these four principles, I find that I become happier and more at peace with myself. It's easier to let go of others; giving of myself is beautifully rewarding in itself; I am increasingly productive; and I am finding within myself a capacity for loving I didn't know I had. Best of all, I no longer need to suffer in order to feel worthwhile.

Kindness Overcomes Inertia

POPE JOHN XIII once said his goal in life was never to be unkind. I liked that, and thought I would also like to make that one of my goals. As I read on about Pope John, I discovered that, though he was kind, he was also firm. He could refuse to do something when he was convinced it was wrong, be truthful even when the truth hurt. Where did he draw the line, I wondered, between being kind and saying and doing things which might hurt other people's feelings?

As I thought about this, and examined my own motives for saying or not saying things, I realized that loving concern for the other's welfare was the important factor in deciding whether or not a word or action is kind. And I also realized that my definition of kindness had been distorted, I'd mistakenly thought that being kind meant not hurting another person's feelings. Consequently, I was easily manipulated by anyone who reacted to something I might say or do by sulking, crying, getting angry, or simply acting hurt. I avoided such confrontations and went to great lengths to avoid controversy.

In Al-Anon, I learned that I had to put my welfare first. That often meant saying or doing things to which the alcoholic had strong negative reactions. He didn't like my saying no, my attending meetings, making friends, doing things by myself. My welfare depended on not removing the painful consequences of his drinking, being honest about my feelings, being firm in the face of angry outbursts and threats. It would have been easy to draw on resentments, anger, self-pity and hatred and to do all these things in a vindictive way. But by having loving concern for my husband's welfare, I could speak the truth, although it was painful for both of us, in the knowledge that, if we were to grow, we both needed to work with reality.

My inability to say how I felt, to make decisions, to refuse to do something I didn't want to do—these all went away as I practiced loving concern for others. Awareness of how I affect others is important. So is weighing what I am about to say or do, its appropriateness, my motives. But I know I am being kind if my behavior is founded on true concern for the other's welfare. Beyond that, I must let go and let the other person work out his or her own feelings.

Honesty Overcomes Depression

DEPRESSION AND I are old acquaintances. Long before I met and married an alcoholic, I had frequent episodes of deep depression, times during which I wished for, or planned my death. The first such time was when I was twelve. Convinced I was a burden to my family, and that everyone would be better off without me, I thought for a long while about committing suicide. Only strong religious beliefs kept me from acting it out.

Feelings of worthlessness and inadequacy plagued me even though, to all appearances, I was quite successful. All through my college years, I perceived life as painful: lonely, frightening, demanding. I longed for an early death.

Marriage to an alcoholic didn't make things any better. My sense of inadequacy increased as all my attempts to make him happy and stop his overdrinking failed. I lost all hope of ever pulling out of my anguish; the despair became unbearable. It was then that Al-Anon entered the picture.

As my ignorance was replaced with knowledge, resentment with understanding, hatred with compassion, confusion with confidence, I began to feel better. At first the difference was so dramatic, I wanted to shout it from the rooftops. However, after about two years in the program, I found myself plunged into another depression, this one just as severe, if not worse, than any I'd ever suffered before. No amount of "Just for Today," "First Things First," or "Let Go and Let God" made me feel better. It was then I realized I needed professional help.

It was in therapy that I learned I was misinterpreting the Al-Anon message. Al-Anon was saying, "Don't argue with him when he's drunk," and I was hearing, "Don't ever express negative feelings." Al-Anon was saying, "What he does is not a reflection on you," and I was hearing, "You're not working your program properly if you get upset by what he says and does." Al-Anon was saying, "Don't nag him about his drinking"; I was hearing, "Don't ever refer to it in any way." Al-Anon was saying, "Act as if you had achieved the qualities you are striving for"; I was hearing, "Don't let him know how you really feel."

I learned that mental health depends on knowing how I feel and being able to express those feelings in a constructive way. I had gotten myself into the awful trap of wanting to be so good at practicing my program, at being so serene and detached, that I was denying my anger, frustration and anxiety most of the time, and feeling guilty about having those kinds of feelings the rest of the time.

Slowly, I began to see that one of the causes of my depression was my inability or unwillingness to be honest about my feelings. Changing what I could in this instance meant changing my attitude toward my feelings.

When I first came into Al-Anon, I *had* to shut my mouth altogether because I wasn't able to say anything constructive. And I *had* to pretend I wasn't worried by going to bed while my husband was still out because I hadn't yet reached the point where I truly had let go of those things over which I had no control.

However, once I got beyond that point—once I could remain calm long enough to think about what I was going to say; once I had enough faith in my Higher Power to let go—I needed to realize that to feel one way and act another is to betray myself and confuse those with whom I am dealing. That is not to say that anything goes! There are appropriate and inappropriate ways of expressing feelings. Emotionally healthy persons are free to choose the method of expression which best suits the occasion because they have fully accepted their feelings as valid.

For instance, if someone says something to me that makes me feel badly, I don't say, "If I were working my program, what he said wouldn't bother me." That would be putting myself down for something over which I have no control. Instead, I wait for an appropriate moment and tell him how he has made me feel. I think it's most unrealistic to expect to be able to live or work with people and never to be bothered at all by anything they do. We would have to be made of stone. The more we care about someone, the more that person's behavior is likely to matter to us. But there's a big difference between having feelings and wanting to control others. It is true that we can't change anyone but ourselves. It is also true we have no right to tell anyone how to live. Manipulation is lack of respect for the other person. However, that is not to say that, in a relationship we ought not have expectations;

that we should never ask for anything; that we should not ever be disappointed.

"I am responsible for my own happiness," means that, if you do something that hurts me or upsets me, I will let you know about it. If you continue to do it, I will do something to change the situation. It means that, if there is something you can do for me which would please me very much, I will let you know. I won't expect you to be a mind reader. If you choose not to do it, I will know more about you than I did before and you will understand me when I tell you I am disappointed. You won't be surprised and say, "Gee, I'm sorry, I didn't know!" We will both know where we stand. I won't be acting like a martyr, trying to make you feel guilty. You will be free to choose whether you want to go on being the way you are, or whether you want to change.

Honest communication is not easy. I am still afraid of rejection, of anger. And, of course, probably the biggest obstacle to my telling you how I really feel is my own shame that I could be so petty or immature, or whatever. I still tend to judge myself and to wish I weren't the way I am sometimes. And if I tell you how I feel, then you will know how I am too. If I tell you how I feel, I am giving you a piece of myself; I am saying that I trust you enough to make myself vulnerable, to take a risk; I am giving you the greatest gift I have to give. I am being my most loving.

Self-Acceptance Replaces Self-Consciousness

WHEN I WAS IN MY teens and twenties, I was very shy. Beige and grey were my favorite colors; I wanted to blend into the background and not be noticed. The fear of making a fool of myself was so great that I never tried anything new. I wouldn't join the school basketball team because I was afraid to make a mistake and be rejected by my teammates. I wouldn't become a cheerleader because I was afraid to appear silly. I couldn't relax on the dance floor and have a good time, so I never became a good dancer. At parties, I was so busy wondering if I would say the wrong thing that I said hardly anything, and could never remember people's names or what they said to me.

I spent hours getting ready to go anywhere because I wanted everything about me to be perfect, and would get very upset if a zipper broke or my hair got messy or anything went wrong with my appearance. I became so terrified of feeling ridiculous that I would walk with my eyes lowered, afraid to look at someone who might not give back a friendly look of recognition, and I never said "Hello" unless the other person greeted me first.

It was impossible for me to ask a question in class, to express an opinion in a group, to relax and have a good time. I couldn't laugh at myself or admit I'd made a mistake. Marriage to an alcoholic only made me worse, because I assumed responsibility for my husband's behavior and felt that *I* looked ridiculous when *he* acted in socially unacceptable ways. I could handle my discomfort only by hiding, or pretending my husband's behavior didn't bother me at all. And of course, I blamed all my unhappiness and shortcomings on him.

In Al-Anon, I was told I couldn't blame the alcoholic for my character defects. My self-consciousness was derived from a poor self-image and the only way I could change that was by changing myself. Encouraged by the loving support of the group, I was able to go through the Fourth and Fifth Steps where I discovered just what my self-image was, and move on to the Seventh, Eighth and Ninth Steps, where I consciously worked on the things I didn't like about myself. The program gently drove home the message that I didn't have to be perfect to be lovable. I was lovable as I was. My only job was to keep on trying to get better.

I learned that I was stuck in a bind: I tried to be perfect in order to be loved, and felt awful when I failed, but at the same time, when I did seem to achieve my goal of perfection, the love I was looking for escaped me. People tend to be turned off by someone who is right all the time and they almost go out of their way to burst the balloon. And so I had to come to grips with the reality that I would never be liked, loved and accepted by everyone, that people would find my mistakes annoying, that I might have to accept someone's anger, but that this is the price we pay for our humanity. And being human entitles me to love and be loved. So often it is our failings that endear us to others.

There were and are three qualities I practice which help me overcome my self-consciousness: enthusiasm, interest in others, and silliness. When I go to a party or a meeting or any place where I am thrown in with strangers, I make a conscious effort to get to know at least one person. Instead of standing there alone, aware that no one is talking to me, I look for someone else who is standing alone, and I go over to them, introduce myself, and ask them about themselves. I get to meet a lot of interesting people that way.

Instead of worrying about failing, I tackle new projects enthusiastically and put my whole self into them. I become so excited about the project, that I forget how I look. The focus is off me.

As for silliness, for me it's a matter of taking risks, having fun. I look silly when I play softball because my children tell me I run funny. I joke and laugh at myself. And I'm even going to learn to ride a bike this year! It's great to let out the little child in me and let her have fun.

Understanding Opens Door to Compassion

I HAVE HEARD that people react to stress in five ways: they placate, blame, intellectualize, become irrelevant, or are congruent. I can certainly identify with that, having done all of them at one time or another.

As the placator, I became the super-martyr, turning myself inside out to please the alcoholic. As the blamer, I laid at his feet the responsibility for all our problems. As the intellectualizer, I read books and spouted theories, well able to discuss anything in the abstract, but totally unable to cope with my real problems. And I became irrelevant when I buried my head like an ostrich, pretending our problems would go away if I ignored them. It was in Al-Anon that I learned to be congruent: to behave appropriately and to deal with my problems instead of playing sick games. And it was here that I gained some understanding of why I'd acted as I did.

I became a martyr and a people-pleaser because this was the way I'd learned to get praise and admiration. I became a blamer when I felt so worthless that I couldn't accept criticism or admit I'd made a mistake for fear that others would see in me what I saw: failure, ineptness, inadequacy. When it became too painful to feel because I took the alcoholic's behavior personally and interpreted it as rejection, I shut my feelings off and became a 'head' person. That is, when I wasn't running away into fantasy because I felt so helpless and unable to cope with reality.

Understanding myself was a big step toward understanding the alcoholic. When I looked at it honestly, I could see that we took turns placating, blaming, intellectualizing and being irrelevant. The same needs that had caused this behavior in me were causing it in him. We weren't so different after all! We did seem to find one type of behavior more comfortable than the others, though, and while my choice most of the time was to placate, his was to blame. By applying what I'd learned about myself to him, I was able to approach him differently.

I learned not to fall into the trap of defending myself or others against false accusations. That was just a waste of time, as was coming back at him with accusations of my own. I learned not to let the alcoholic set my goals for me. Living up to my own expectations was enough. When confronted with a verbal attack, I would try to stay calm and remember that it was his self-hatred, guilt and fear of being uncovered in all his humanness that caused his need to blame. Instead of becoming embroiled in a heated argument over whose fault it was, I would try to focus on the problem itself.

It wasn't easy. I still felt angry and frustrated sometimes. But understanding the behavior permitted some compassion to seep through so that I could be less defensive and more objective.

Learning From Experience

As LONG AS I remained locked in my need to appear perfect, I couldn't grow because I couldn't look at my mistakes. Thank goodness Al-Anon has helped me to look at criticisms as opportunities for growth. I would hate to be condemned to repeat my mistakes forever, as the expression goes, because I'd neglected to learn from them. Keeping an open mind allows other points of view to come through and be weighed against mine, and I almost always learn from listening to others.

I know, too, that when I'm trying to communicate ideas, I have to be sure the people who are listening to me define the words I'm using the same way I do, or there will be misunderstanding. One time, I designed a brochure for the hospital where I work, describing an educational program in alcoholism. One of the lectures was on family patterns of behavior, and I used the words 'How to stop enabling.' In Al-Anon, this has a very special connotation. It means that we must stop trying to protect the alcoholic from the painful consequences of his drinking, even to the point of allowing a crisis to happen. However, to psychologists and other people in the helping professions, it has an altogether different meaning.

One day, I got an irate phone call from the hospital administrator saying, "We're supposed to be enablers! What do you mean, 'Stop enabling?' " I was reminded in less than pleasant terms, if I'm going to use words or expressions that have an accepted meaning in an unusual way, I should put them in quotation marks. He was right, of course. To him, 'enabling' means helping people help themselves.

We sometimes get so used to using words that we forget their meaning might not be so clear to others, and this can happen even within Al-Anon. This month, for instance, we received two letters asking "What are the *principles* of Al-Anon that we're supposed to 'practice in all our affairs'? " I'd always thought these were self-evident, and proceeded to answer the letters, telling the writers that the Steps contained the principles of surrender (First and Third), faith (Second and Eleventh), trust (Fifth), humility (Fourth and Fifth), fairness (Ninth), honesty (Fourth and Ninth), and brotherhood (Twelfth) among others. And then I realized that this is the way *I* see it! Perhaps others view the Steps and principles of Al-Anon quite differently. Who am I to spell it out for someone else?

Surrender vs Self-Will

WHEN I WAS A little child, I loved to play school, and I always wanted to be the teacher. Those who knew me well sometimes teased me by calling me 'Mother Superior,' indicating no doubt that they had noticed my tendency to be bossy. Even then, I liked being in charge and having things my way.

As I grew up, I found it so easy to criticize others. Among my favorite fantasies were images of how I would do things *if I were they:* how I would discipline that child; how I would run that hospital floor; how I would decorate that house; and so on. When I got married, I had a lot of preconceived notions about what marriage ought to be and how husbands ought to behave. Being alcoholic, my husband had many head-on collisions with my notions carved in stone, and the war was on. But I was fighting something much bigger than I could know.

The more I fought, the more I manipulated, the more I tried to get things to go *my* way, the more frustrated I became until, totally defeated, I found Al-Anon. Here I discovered that we win by giving up. We become capable of directing our destiny by surrendering to a will other than our own. We take hold of our lives by letting go.

It sounds like a riddle, almost like double-talk. But it's true. The key to freedom is the placing of our lives and wills into the care of someone else, that someone, of course, being our trustworthy Higher Power. Once I surrendered my will, my whole life and my whole attitude toward it changed. First of all, I didn't have to win any more. There was no war. When I surrendered my will to my Higher Power, I didn't submit to a fatalistic philosophy of impotence. Instead, I subscribed to the idea that, by doing my best and what's best for me, I was doing God's will. In a very real sense, then, I became able to direct my destiny because I became free to act in my own best interest. By doing God's will, I became my most potent, most productive self. The need to change other people and the responsibility for their behavior were no longer in the way.

This principle of surrender can be applied in every area of my life. When I serve on a committee, I can offer my opinions and ideas without feeling crushed, put down or angry if the decision of the group goes the other way. In my job I can do my best without looking for praise or appreciation and I can make decisions about my career, daring to venture in new, untried areas, without being afraid. At home, I can allow my relatives to live according to their values, even when that implies rejection of me, without being upset.

Surrender has made me free.

Accentuating the Positive

REMEMBER THE MUNSTER FAMILY on television? Lily always used to get a laugh when she talked about her 'weed garden.' Most people don't like weeds, and many spend a lot of time and money each year getting rid of crabgrass and other unsightly, unwanted growths. But not everyone looks at weeds the same way. Ever since I read a book that was sent to me by the Museum of Natural History, in which the author talks about the beauty of our wildflowers, I have looked at weeds in a new light.

I see that the world is filled with beauty, and each weed has its own, special, charming quality. In fact, each November I enjoy gathering armfuls of dried weeds and grasses and filling my house with golden bouquets of God's generous bounty. It's a matter of looking at the positive, and it makes all the difference in the world.

It's so easy to get into the habit of negative thinking. Our parents correct our mistakes, our teachers indicate our errors, we get into trouble for the things we do wrong, and sometimes it seems we are surrounded by people who are ready to pounce on our smallest mistake. In turn, we become negative too, completing the circle. We tell ourselves we're no good, that we can't do it, that no one will like it, that we're inadequate.

We find fault with our children, our spouses, our group, our community, our society. Have you ever kept track of how often you say 'can't, don't, won't, shouldn't' in relation to yourself or others?

It doesn't cost anything to notice what someone is doing right, how well someone looks, how hard someone is trying. And it pays tremendous dividends. Not only does it make others feel as though they've been stroked with a piece of soft fur or velvet; it helps us to appreciate them and be glad for whatever it is they are adding to our lives.

We can stress the positive in our work and other endeavors as well. True, it's important for us to see what isn't right and try to correct it. But it's equally important for us to evaluate our gains and feel the good feelings that come from accomplishment.

The conscious practice of positive thinking, of telling ourselves we're worthwhile, of recognizing our qualities, helps us to stay self-assured, comfortable and pleasant. It makes it easier for us to be more creative, to keep an open mind, to be receptive to new approaches.

Having a positive attitude is very close to, and an important part of, becoming willing to have God remove our defects. We tell ourselves we want to change, that we can change, that we will change, that we will get better. And we become open to the sunlight of God's love and wisdom when we lift the blinds of negative thought, cynicism, bitterness, defeatism, rigidity and prejudice.

The constant practice of Al-Anon principles enables us to hear brilliant insights in the words of the uneducated, to find love in criticism, to be helped by those we're helping and taught by those we're teaching. We can learn to see beauty in the most dismal surroundings, in the wrinkles on an aged faced, in the mold on an old brick. A positive attitude is a great blessing.

The Christmas Spirit

THE JOY ON THE face of a child Christmas morning is something most parents wake up early to see, even though they may have gone to bed very late the night before. We all enjoy receiving gifts and being surprised by a thoughtful gesture. But pleasant as it is to be remembered and to receive tokens of affection from those who love us, the joy of receiving can't compare to the joy of giving.

I remember the first Christmas my children were old enough to have saved, shopped, wrapped and hidden gifts for other family members. Suddenly they were more interested in watching other people open their gifts than in opening their own. The keen excitement of knowing they had made or prepared a gift that would bring pleasure just lit up their little faces. And the happiness that glowed in their eyes when the gift was finally opened was more beautiful than any look they'd ever had. They had discovered the joy of giving.

Among the happiest people I know are those whose lives are dedicated to helping others. Down deep inside all of us is the need to have a purpose, to lead meaningful lives. Many of us find that being of service to others fills this need. Certainly we are given many opportunities to be of service in Al-Anon: as group officers, sponsors, speakers, or as volunteers on some special project. Of course, there are many ways of giving. We can give of our money, our time, our energy. But most rewarding of all is the gift of self; the sharing with each other our experience, pain and growth. As we give of ourselves in this way, we discover that nothing is more rewarding than the work we do for nothing.

Al-Anon teaches us to practice the Christmas spirit all through the year. By not reserving our generosity and our giving to this short season, we carry each day in our hearts the lightness and happiness that traditionally belong to this special time.

Although we might be able to maintain this giving spirit throughout the year, it sometimes happens that we find it difficult to apply it at Christmas time in our own homes. Our expectations of what Christmas 'ought' to be, and the anticipation of problems may make us tense, irritable and upset.

I can remember one Christmas when beset by financial problems, and besieged by almost daily crises, I just couldn't seem to get into the 'Christmas spirit.' I had no inclination to shop, to decorate, to cook. Lost in self-pity, I thought, 'Why bother? No one will visit us. No one will enjoy it anyway.'

A wise friend reminded me that this was the children's Christmas, too. As blue and as down as I felt, it was important for me to try to make a nice Christmas for them. And so, getting out of myself, I concentrated on doing what I could to make it as pleasant as possible for my three youngsters.

I had to overcome my preconceived notions of what we had to have in order to have a good holiday: lots of guests, piles of gifts, freedom from crises. Instead, I had to reorder my priorities. Making special treats became more important than buying gifts. Decorating to please the children and allowing them to help became more important than creating stunning decorative designs to impress visitors. Maintaining a climate of emotional stability in the face of continuing crises became more important than trying to avoid the crises. My values changed because they had to, and I learned a lot from that.

Before I knew it, I was feeling myself being buoyed up by the excitement of anticipation, the joy of giving, the delight of planning delights for others. I got over my depression, and we all had a good Christmas in spite of our problems.

Whatever your situation may be this year, I hope you will be encouraged by the thought that, by applying Al-Anon principles to your daily life, you, too, can have a good Christmas. I wish all of you the joys of self-discovery and fulfillment, the peace of knowing that you are in God's care, the healing balm of love, and the spiritual rewards of service and giving.

Hildegard M. V.
Editor 1977–1983

"*The FORUM* is a channel of sharing for Al-Anon and Alateen members throughout the world. Anyone who has ever said anything at a meeting has something to contribute to this monthly meeting on paper."

Out of Darkness

EIGHT-YEAR OLD JIMMY riding from his home in northern New Jersey to New York City on a train became anxious when it entered a tunnel. The sudden blackness outside the windows, the feeling of being confined and fear that the darkness would never end, terrified him. Each time he was taken into the city he was more frightened so that the trip, even if it was for a pleasant outing such as visiting the zoo, became a nightmare.

One day his father took him for a long walk on a nearby mountain. From that vantage point the boy could see where the tracks entered the tunnel and also where they came out. Suddenly he had a totally different perspective. He realized that there was a beginning and an end to the dark stretch and he need not be afraid.

When we feel that our lives are engulfed in such a murky tunnel we need to gain that same perspective. We can overcome the rising panic as the black seems to be closing in, if we realize that there are tracks leading us through and out of the darkness.

The Slogans and Steps of Al-Anon are the rails that can carry us along until we again reach the light. Each time we apply them to a difficult situation we are progressing, we are moving forward.

Even if we are still figuratively sitting in the same seat in the same coach of the same train, we are in a totally different position when we change both our attitudes and our actions. Suddenly we'll find that the view outside the window is bright again.

Heavenly Lights

'HUMILITY LIKE DARKNESS reveals heavenly lights,' wrote Henry David Thoreau in *Walden.*

Standing in a clearing in the woods on a bright summer day, the straight trunks and deep green branches of the pines and the white bark and lacy green leaves of the birches stand out against the azure blue of the sky. The closeness of the trees fills our foreground. We hear the bird calls and the murmuring water of a brook and feel very much a part of the forest.

That same clearing at night presents a completely different picture and evokes totally new feelings. In the dark stillness our eyes are drawn past the shadowy clumps of trees to the hundreds of stars high above them. A feeling of awe and wonder and joy at the majesty of the scene fills us.

The stars were always there, but during the day the bright sun obliterated their light. In the same way, the beams of our self-will obscure the light available to us from a Higher Power. Without our awareness of that source, without our willingness to stop and listen to something beyond ourselves, we are cut off from the broader perspective and the help available to us.

Humility and the willingness to follow higher guidance are very much a part of the Al-Anon program. Many of the Steps direct us to have this attitude. But humility doesn't mean to negate our own selves. In the forest clearing every plant, tree and bird has a part and plays its role. We also have a role to play and have our own unique function. We do count. And it is with true humility and the understanding that we are a part of the greater whole that we can reach out to contact our Higher Power and see those heavenly lights.

Living Free

WHAT DOES THE SLOGAN, 'Keep it Simple,' mean? How can it help?

The dictionary defines simple as *free from* pretense, *free from* vanity, *free of* complications, *free from* elaboration. In other words—simplicity can give us freedom.

When we are free from pretense, we can be open in our relationships. We need not continue the old cover-up and denial of the problem of alcoholism. We won't fail to say what needs to be said directly, honestly and—hopefully—lovingly to the alcoholic, other members of our family and friends. We can face the situation of our lives straight on and deal with it as it is, without pretending it's not there, that it's either better or worse than it actually is, or that it will just go away if we ignore it.

When we are free from vanity we don't have an inflated idea of what we can do. We stop trying to run the show. We keep our hands off. We don't think that we caused the drinking and we don't expend our energy uselessly trying to stop it.

Is it ever possible to free our lives of complications? How we confuse ourselves with thinking in circles, our tangled relationships with others, our pressures of time and space. I love to walk in the woods and reduce worldly possessions in my pocket to a key, a comb and a Kleenex. Why can't I keep my life that simple more often? My attic, with wall to wall objects, kept me in one place much longer than necessary. When I moved from my roomy house to a small apartment, I whittled my belongings down drastically but I still kept much too much. My closets, drawers and cupboards are overflowing with the extra this, the special that, to use or wear or cook in, in some unlikely circumstance.

Material things are a burden; they keep life complicated. I'm sure God has no cluttered cupboards. Maybe that's what heaven is all about. If ever all my drawers, closets and bookshelves were neat and orderly I'd surely think I was living in heaven.

Using the basic ideas of the program—free from elaboration—will bring me as close as possible to that ideal. Al-Anon's message is a fundamental approach to living—we learn to admit our powerlessness, to turn to a Higher Power, and to change our attitudes and actions. Though that is tremendously profound, it is also beautifully simple.

Reducing our emotions, possessions, concepts and time, to essentials—simplifying our lives—will help us to live more freely and happily and grow more easily in the program.

Warning: Emotional Danger

'PLEASE DON'T FEED THE animals,' 'Watch your step,' 'Cross at crosswalks,' 'Don't Enter,' 'Danger: Thin ice,' 'Fasten seatbelts.'

All day long we're bombarded with admonitions but we forge blithely ahead, headstrong, ignoring them—and get bitten, bumped, battered and bruised.

Two incidents recently caught me up short. Lighting a match in my kitchen the other night, the whole matchbook suddenly went up in flames, singeing my fingers before I could toss it into the sink. 'Close cover before striking matches,' is a warning that means something to me now.

The next event contained a greater element of danger. Canoeing down the Delaware River on a lovely sunny day when the river seemed calm, we cavalierly didn't wear the life preservers and used them only as cushions. When the canoe hit a sudden stretch of white water, we nearly tipped over and got swept away in the current. Fortunately, the canoe stayed right side up and we were soon floating smoothly downstream again.

How often we also ignore or misuse the warnings given to us to handle our emotional lives. Why can't I remember the slogan, Think, before I make that thoughtless and possibly wounding remark, or before I agree to a plan of action that's not what I really want to do? If I would take a minute to stop and think before I rushed heart-first into a situation, I'd avoid getting into a spot where I'm likely to be burned.

How easily I misuse the slogan, Let Go and Let God. It doesn't mean that I can sit idly by and trust that somehow everything will work out fine. I can't let go of my responsibilities. I can't expect God to do my ironing or 'hoe my potatoes'. To use the slogan properly, I let go of other people's responsibilities, realizing that I weaken them if I don't allow them the opportunity to take care of their own affairs. I shouldn't build up my own ego by jumping in and handling what is not my business.

In the same way, I must let go of what is beyond me in my own life; let God direct the larger perimeters of it, trusting that if I take care of my everyday needs, make proper use of the duties and opportunities that come my way, I will be able to meet the critical emergencies.

Realistic Expectations

'IF I DIDN'T HAVE expectations, my heart would never be broken,' someone said recently at a meeting.

What are the expectations that break our hearts? The phone that doesn't ring—the kind word that isn't said—the job that doesn't come through—the strong hand that isn't offered. So often they are the actions we expect from another person.

Wishing for others to fulfill our desires is futile. More often than not, it sets us up for frustration as we try to cajole or force them into meeting our needs. We sit by the phone expectantly, we count on having situations work out the way we'd like them to, we look for someone else's behavior to change in order to make our lives so much happier.

In Al-Anon, though, we learn that we can change no one but ourselves. Are our expectations of ourselves reasonable? Do we bitterly condemn ourselves for not meeting impossible standards and then throw up our hands in despair as we decide we're just not good enough: 'Why did I say that?' 'If only I hadn't done that!' 'Why can't I ever remember to . . .?'

Seeing ourselves, others, and the situation we're in realistically, can temper our expectations, keep us from hoping for explicit miracles. At the same time that we release ourselves from the tyranny of looking for something specific to happen, we can anticipate so much more. We can have larger expectations. We needn't look for a blue suit to come next Tuesday, but we can have faith that next week we will be amply clothed. The change in our attitude will ease our strain and help us to see the bounties available to us.

In our relationships with others, we can't expect that a change in our attitude and response to someone will automatically result in an immediately rewarding conversation. With our hurt children, for example, we must first build up trust, give them time to find us believable. But we can have faith that if we keep giving undemanding love to them, the change in our approach will, over a period of time, work toward an understanding between us.

Our expectations are often our way of issuing orders to God, of hoping to bend the rainbow to end at our feet. Through expectations we live unrealistically in the future; we're robbed of the ability to live fully today. When we let go of the tension of programming what we want to have happen and trust that something larger is available to us, we open ourselves to the good that can come our way.

Affordable Gifts

FINDING THE RIGHT PRESENT for each person on our holiday gift list can be particularly worrisome when we don't have enough money to buy what we'd like. What are the gifts we can give that won't overdraw our bank account now and for which we won't be billed after the holidays?

First of all we can give the gift of patience. Standing in line at the checkout counter we can help the harried sales clerk and ease our own urgency if we take it easy and manage to be patient. Bringing patience and courtesy home with us along with the mince meat and cranberries and serving them generously can make life much more pleasant. Our spouse, no matter whether drunk or sober, would be sure to welcome a good portion of patience from us.

Whether they've asked for it or not, our children have high on their list of wishes the gift of freedom—the permission to live their own lives without our directing, demanding, interfering. No matter what their age, we can let them live without our petty tyranny. When we give them loving independence we demonstrate our trust in them; we give them the opportunity to realize their own self-worth.

The gift of acceptance acknowledges each person's right to be himself. We let go of our inflexible judgmental attitudes; we stop trying to reshape everyone into our mold. This certainly need not open us up to accepting unacceptable behavior or condoning unkind actions. What it can do is keep us from running the entire show according to our script and defining each actor's role as we see it.

During the holidays we want frivolous gifts and that's where hugs, kisses and laughter come in. They're the sunbeams and stars that hang on the Christmas tree and light up the whole house when they're given lavishly and lovingly.

But sometimes it seems as though we're doing all the giving. Why doesn't someone give gifts to us? There's a paradox here.

When we give for the pure joy of giving with no thought of return, then it flows back to us and the wise words in the prayer of St. Francis come true: 'It is in giving that we receive.'

We receive relaxation and serenity when we give patience and practice easy does it. We find time and energy to enjoy our own lives when we let others live fully and freely. We realize a much larger enjoyment and appreciation of others and of ourselves when we let go, give tolerance and practice acceptance.

It's Christmas all year long when we give what we learn through the program.

The Reality Of What Is

WHAT'S THE MOST HELPFUL tool I can take with me into the New Year? It could be one simple word—just two letters— IS.

If I can truly face what *is* in my life and my world, I'll know where I am—not see it the way I'd like it to be. I'll stop living in the unreal past or in the fantasy future. I'll know the true situation—the first step in coping with it.

Often we look back and take as the present reality what we remember of what *was,* instead of seeing it like it *is.* It doesn't matter whether we use a big black brush to paint a scene darker, even worse than it actually was, or if we use a gold magic marker to draw the happy picture we would like it to have been. Either way, when we base what we do on our view of the past instead of what is now, we're not responding appropriately. When we carry the hurts of the past into today, refuse to see how someone has changed—either for better or for worse—when we believe that our reactions must keep the same pattern, we aren't dealing with what *is.* We're playing the same old tapes.

We also distort what *is* by longing for what could have been, or what could still be—if only. That's living in an unreality that robs us of the ability to proceed from where we are. It's so easy to indulge in wishful thinking, 'If only he or she would do this or that. . .' or 'If only I had . . . or could . . . or knew this or that.'

'If wishes were horses, beggars would ride,' so goes the old saying. Wishing in vain robs us of energy—energy we need to handle the reality of the present.

So Happy New Year to us all. When we can see the coming year and all that it brings, and can face it as it *is*, then it will be a constructive growing year for us.

Seeing With Love-Filled Eyes

THE HEARTS, FLOWERS and paper lace of Valentine's Day aren't enough. We all want to be loved more than that. Nothing is as richly satisfying as a one-to-one relationship with someone who cares for us and who shares our thoughts and feelings. When we have that, the whole world lights up and everything seems possible.

But, how seldom it happens, and even less often does it last. We are so often alone—either physically separated or estranged from those near us. What can we do during those long lonesome times when we are without love, but still need love?

We can learn to find it in other ways: talking to children, enjoying the roses in a neighbor's garden, feeding some birds, cuddling the baby in the downstairs apartment, sharing at Al-Anon meetings our hurts and joys and those of others.

At first it's a matter of keeping busy, but not in a frantic running away from an empty apartment or a loveless home. It's finding within us the things to fulfill ourselves that we enjoy. When we meet friends, both old and new, who share those things, it's an extension of ourselves and a deepening of perception. The world is alive and so are we.

When there are disappointments and I have to go back to square one—back to the birds and roses—I know if I keep growing and allowing myself to stay vulnerable, I can love and be loved again.

In a prayer I often say in the morning, there's a line 'Help me to view the world today with love-filled eyes.' That's the secret. If we feel love inside us, the world has so many more possibilities. We're not searching the horizon for that knight in shining armor but find happiness in many different ways.

And if we still need to hear the words 'I love you' we can always find all the sentiments on a beautiful valentine and send it to ourselves.

Truly Unselfish

'I'm No. 1.' How many of us can say that without feeling guilty? Should we consider our own wants and needs? Do we even know what they are?

We sometimes hear that Al-Anon is a selfish program. There are many ways of interpreting that. A major one is that Al-Anon helps us to discover our own self, often after years of self-denial and self-humiliation.

We begin to recognize we can be good to ourselves. It's often as basic as eating a good meal whether or not the alcoholic eats with us, getting enough sleep even if the alcoholic wants to continue talking or arguing all night, and following our own interests of reading or visiting friends even if the alcoholic is glued to the TV screen. It includes taking care of our appearance, not denying ourselves the clothes or the grooming that would give our spirits a lift. It means using money to buy what is important for us and our family instead of covering liquor bills.

At a recent meeting a newcomer asked how she could plan a vacation when she didn't know if her alcoholic husband would be willing or able to go. She was told to make the plans that would please her and hope he would be able to accompany her. She was to do what was best for her.

Our goal isn't me-first-mania, but a belief in our rights and worth. It doesn't give us the right to ride roughshod over other people's feelings or try to make others look bad. In the same way, we shouldn't be insensitive to our own needs or deny our feelings. We must acknowledge ourselves before we can become healed and whole. When we can think of ourselves as No. 1—not with prideful vanity, but with wholesome humility—then we have come a long way in gaining our self-respect.

But this Al-Anon self-help program enables us to go even further. We don't find ourselves merely to stay on the level of self-centeredness and self-gratification. We can, once we know ourselves, reach out to others and become part of the larger community. We reinforce ourselves even more by helping others. We can learn to love our neighbor as ourselves. That is a truly unselfish program.

Courage To Risk

WHAT ARE THE REGRETS that hurt us the most? While we don't want to dwell on the past, looking back can help us learn from our mistakes to improve our present.

In that past, our regret so often is about things we haven't done: the job opportunity we didn't grasp; the time we didn't offer a hand to someone in need; the trip, venture or friendship we were timid about pursuing, or the constructive action we were afraid to take.

Often it is our fear of risk that keeps us immobilized. Fear must be distinguished from caution. Caution is essential before we launch a new endeavor, head in an unfamiliar direction, explore an untried path; we must anticipate and face the possible consequences. But when we aren't willing to consider alternatives, are too afraid of possible failures, too frightened of the social consequences, too timid and worried to move at all, we handicap and limit ourselves.

Having the courage to risk and even possibly to fail builds our self-respect. If we feel right about ourselves, strong in our rights and beliefs, then we can go ahead. We won't feel we are personally a failure if something doesn't work out.

Building self-respect—so often that's the hardest of all. Working the Steps of the Al-Anon program, learning to see ourselves and our situation with honest clarity, and strengthening our relationship with our Higher Power, can give us the feeling within that is self-esteem.

Then we'll have a clearer view of ourselves and our world and we'll be able to do whatever needs to be done. We can speak to someone about what troubles us. We can take that course at an adult school. We can call the police. We can risk living. We won't be frozen into inaction; we will have the strength of our convictions and we'll be able to express them lovingly.

When we aren't afraid to risk today, we are less likely to have regrets tomorrow.

Don't Fence Me In

THE OTHER DAY I noticed a horse looking across a low rail fence to a brook as though he wished he could cross over and drink from it. Actually, if he had only realized it, he could easily have jumped the fence.

I began to think—how many fences hold us back? Fences we could surmount? Fences we have built ourselves?

We fence ourselves in when we tell ourselves we're not capable enough to accomplish something; we're not worthy enough to deserve what we want; we're not brave enough to attempt a task. Those are mental barriers constructed by our fears, but they restrain us as cruelly as barbed-wire barricades.

In Al-Anon we learn to change our feelings about ourselves. We see that our limitations are often imposed on us not by outward circumstances but by our mental attitudes, the beliefs we hold about ourselves. In Al-Anon we begin to lower the bars on those rail fences. We begin to realize what we can do, what we deserve.

Sometimes when we feel boxed in but don't know where we want to go or what we want to do, we needn't try to jump over the fence and dash off someplace right then. It might be time for us to do nothing but restore our inner reserves. Those quiet periods will serve a purpose, especially if we don't rage against them but make each day as good and satisfying as possible.

That's part of the process of getting to know and accept our true and best self. It will help us demolish the self-imposed, self-defeating views of ourselves. Then we will no longer be held back by our negative beliefs. We'll know we can leap over those fences.

Sermons in Stones

Sweet are the uses of adversity. . .
And this our life. . .
Finds tongues in trees,
Books in the running brooks,
Sermons in stones and good in every thing.
Shakespeare. As You Like It

Finding good in everything doesn't mean pretending our troubles don't exist, glossing them over with platitudes or being long-suffering.

There is something we can do, however. Adversity is defined as a disastrous experience that can result in mental or physical distress. When alcoholism comes into our lives, it brings, or is, adversity. Al-Anon helps us to overcome it. Studying the Steps and practicing the principles enables us to deal with the problems alcoholism brings and heal our mental and physical distress. With a change in our attitude and actions, we find "tongues in trees" and "sermons in stones." We see we would not have matured without overcoming the adversity.

On my bookshelf is a small black stone I keep to remind me of this. I picked it up a few years ago, on a beautiful Caribbean beach. I had been talking with friends about what we wanted to take back from this idyllic vacation. Having just moved to a small apartment, I didn't want to clutter it with a single additional possession so I chose to bring back a memory: the view of the ocean from my room. That way I could always have sunshine.

"Won't it ever rain on your view?" my good friends asked. Petulantly I replied "It's my view and I can make it anything I want." They persisted and asked "What about nighttime?" Grudgingly I conceded that the tropical night with stars could also be beautiful.

The next morning while walking on the beach I picked up pebbles and held in my hand a pink, a white, a yellowish and a black one. "I don't want that somber stone" I said and tossed it on the sand. Just as a wave washed it back into the ocean, I suddenly understood.

Everything can't always be bright and beautiful. It's childish to pretend that it is. Seeing the reality of our lives, even the dark parts, and dealing with them maturely can make life sweet. I waded into the water and miraculously found again the small dark "sermon in stone."

Quietness

A LETTER TO *The FORUM* quoted Robert E. Lee who said of a friend "There was a quietness in that man's mind, the quietness of heavenly wisdom and . . . willingness to obey present duty."

The Al-Anon member sees our program as a means to gain those attributes. His comments led me—as often happens when I read letters that come across my desk—to a deeper understanding of the principles of Al-Anon.

"Willingness to obey present duty" embodies application of so many Steps and slogans. It means being ready to do whatever task is at hand. It means having the humility to see the reality of the present and respond to it responsibly. It means changing our attitude from self-willed defiance to acceptance—of the unchangeable, never of the unacceptable.

We cannot make these distinctions without quietness, and a deep quietness is the pathway to "heavenly wisdom." Even living in a confused and tumultuous situation we can treasure moments of quietness to sooth our soul. They can come to us in the beauty of nature or a friendly smile.

When we flail out in vain against the wind and tides and fight the forces we cannot change, we lose touch with the infinite, with the power beyond, with the God of our understanding. Going with the current, working with the wind, can take us out of turmoil to a quiet place. Our mind becomes calm and still.

In that quiet we can hear the seed of our self-knowledge growing within us, we can hear the humming of the stars and the heartbeat of the world.

Sorrow

LAST SUMMER WE had a sad loss at the World Service Office; Tony, who had been with us for seven years, died very suddenly. When a young man who has so many fine attributes dies, it is a wrench for all those who knew him.

In the first days following his death, when we were all still unbelieving that Tony would no longer be there to take care of sending the mail to members all over the world, we held our regular weekly Al-Anon meeting at lunch hour. The topic of the meeting was One Day at a Time and as each person spoke, Tony was much in everyone's thoughts.

We realized how important it is to let people know we care about them. So often we don't take the time in a busy schedule to really talk with and be with a person. We began to look at one another and think how we can make every encounter with the people we meet throughout the day more worthwhile. As someone said, "Let's not be slipshod about each day." By making each day more meaningful, without regrets for yesterday or worrying about tomorrow, we can find more joy.

Just as we can know joy, we must also at times experience sorrow. There are many kinds of sorrow. In addition to loss or separation, there is the death of our hopes and dreams. It often involves many emotions—grief, anger, depression, guilt. The way to surmount them is to let go of the pain. When we put all our energies into the past and into our regrets, we continue to give them strength to hurt us. We can instead concentrate on the good in the situation, the experience or the person and take that good with us into the future.

It is always hard to let go of someone we have loved or something that is meaningful in our lives. Facing the uncompromising finality of an ending, acknowledging the reality of it, brings a deep hurt. We need to admit it, mourn it, experience our emotions fully, and then go on. The time comes to realize, "This too shall pass." We can be comforted. If we let go of it and we allow the pain to ease, the time will come when we can look back happily remembering with only a gentle sorrow.

Cleaning Up a Mess

HOW DO WE CLEAN up a mess? I had to figure that out recently and it took me a while, but I learned from it.

When I came back from my vacation, I not only had all the laundry and regular unpacking to deal with, I also found my apartment upset. A good friend of mine had given her daughter the key to my apartment to help out friends of hers, a couple of newlyweds who had no place to go for their honeymoon. That would have been all right with me, but they didn't respect my home.

The disorder of misplaced things and sloppy housekeeping on top of jet lag was too much to face. I just couldn't cope with it right away. When I tried to vacuum, I was pushing a mountain of resentment along with the machine. It was exhausting. My suitcase stayed partially unpacked.

One morning, after I had gone to an Al-Anon meeting the night before, and had an extra long night's sleep, I woke up with my head much clearer. I whipped through the apartment cleaning up and putting things back into place. Suddenly it was easy and I wondered why.

Then I realized it was easy because I had finally cleaned up the mess in my head. Dumping my resentment and resting up had changed my attitude both mentally and physically.

That's the Al-Anon message. When we change our attitude we can deal with our problems constructively. Whether it's ordinary housekeeping chores, the chaos of conflicting plans and schedules, the jumble of holiday wrappings or the muddle of our emotions, we can find the thread to untangle the mess if we straighten out our thinking with the help of first things first and easy does it—but do it!

Step One . . .

We admitted we were powerless over alcohol—that our lives had become unmanageable.

Admitting our powerlessness over alcohol, actually letting go, takes some of us a long, long time. While we still allow our moods to be influenced by the sobriety or lack of it in our homes, while we only tentatively let go of trying to control another person, while we haltingly grope for an understanding of our Higher Power, our lives continue to be unmanageable.

Even after we start to grow by applying the Al-Anon program there are days when we feel the same exhaustion, inertia and indecision of the pre-Al-Anon years. That's when it's time to remember we can keep our lives manageable by taking all the overwhelming responsibilities one day at a time. Take them one hour at a time!

One day, when I felt completely bogged down with those helpless feelings pouring down on me, a good Al-Anon friend made an excellent suggestion. She said to take a pile of black checkers and mentally assign each one a task. Then when I had washed a window, written a letter, or planned a menu and shopping list, I could move a checker to the 'done' pile.

Also, she said to intersperse the black checkers with red ones. 'Give yourself the time to walk around the block, read that magazine you've set aside, take a luxurious, soaking, meditative bath. The situation isn't unmanageable,' she pointed out. 'You are!'

Tackling our own lives, putting some order into them and regaining a positive attitude toward our responsibilities will free us from confusion. With a new perspective, we'll be able to throw off any guilt we might be assuming about the alcoholism. We'll stop being obsessed by alcohol and then be able to realize we are powerless over it.

Step Two . . .

Came to believe that a Power greater than ourselves could restore us to sanity.

The first three words of this Step are a statement of movement—a going forward. They embody the idea of progress and don't demand a full-blown belief to start us on the return to sanity. Sanity in the Al-Anon sense means a feeling of serenity, of purpose and manageability in our lives.

Each member can take that step forward—of coming to believe—at his own pace, in his own direction. The atheist in full denial of any deity, the agnostic in disbelief, the Christian, Hindu, Moslem or the member of any other faith will each, as a result of this Step, have a different understanding of the power that is important in his life.

The Al-Anon program is spiritual, not religious. We each have the freedom to believe what we choose. It does not matter what power we take, if we recognize one greater than our own ego. For many, especially at first, it is the Al-Anon group itself. One member started off considering the Fifth Avenue bus as his Higher Power because it took him from where he was to where he wanted to go—certainly a very useful definition of purpose.

It is helpful, however, to realize that we can invest the power in which we place our belief with many different attributes. Do we see anger and retribution in this power? Or love and compassion? If our view is limited by negative emotions we can search further and find another path or another view of our power that will help us to 'come to believe.'

Step Three . . .

Made a decision to turn our will and our lives over to the care of God as we understood Him.

Making decisions was often agonizingly difficult for many of us in the days before Al-Anon. Or if we made them, we were motivated so often by destructive emotions that our actions only led us deeper into problems.

The Third Step, which calls for the most important decision of all, seems to ask too much of us when we are new in Al-Anon. Yet when we can take that Step, everything else seems to fall into place.

This is not to say that from then on God decides for us whether to have peas or beans for dinner, or whether we should go to the movies or go bowling. It gives us a firm faith that we can trust a larger power and that answers will come more easily when we do.

This Step can be construed as making a decision to accept the reality of our lives rather than continuing to impose our own idea of what our lives should be. We stop playing the role of God. Once we give up our self-willed small egos and realize we cannot control and manipulate our world, we feel a tremendous relief. We can relax; we don't have to be the Big Thumb, we let the real God take over.

We also realize that the world does not hang on our petty decisions. It will continue to spin, and our lives will go on even if we make a wrong decision. Any determination we make is for today. Tomorrow, with fresh insight, we may act or think differently. But we can meet a situation and decide how to deal with it, instead of remaining paralyzed, afraid to move for fear of making a mistake.

Turning our life and will over to the care of God as we understand Him gives us the greatest freedom of all—the freedom to act with faith.

Step Four . . .

Made a searching and fearless moral inventory of ourselves.
What exactly is a moral inventory? According to definition it is a listing of our character traits and patterns of conduct from the point of view of right and wrong.

But what is wrong? In Al-Anon we try not to judge others. We even learn not to condemn ourselves harshly. Most of us, however, have standards of behavior that we consider right and proper. We may think we are living according to those standards when actually, due to the distortions of living with alcoholism, we have strayed far from our ideals.

Honesty is one of the ideal virtues we probably think we uphold. We may even be scrupulous in observing some aspects of it—like returning an overpayment of money. But, in hiding from the truth of our situation, in denying the reality of our problem, are we actually living a lie? The error in our conduct here may not be considered sinful but it is wrong if what we are doing makes matters worse.

In taking this Fourth Step inventory it can be productive to use that test of right or wrong—Is it helping?

Is our self-pity helping us cope with our life situation?

Is our resentment easing our tensions?

Is our berating of the alcoholic leading him or her to self-awareness, or improving our own?

Of course not. Then why do we continue in this destructive course? When the Fourth Step inventory helps us realize the futility of our actions and the negativeness of our dispositions, we have the opportunity to make a useful about-face.

Tearing out our bad habits of thought or action can be difficult unless we make a conscious effort to replace them. Nursing along a good habit or thought can eventually crowd out the bad.

When we fill our minds with gratitude for even the smallest good in each day, there will be less room for self-pity.

When we learn to forgive, not to judge, and to change what we can change, we need no longer harbor resentments.

When we detach with love from the behavior of the alcoholic and learn to live our own lives, we begin to halt the downward spiral of despair.

These right actions will not only make our days much more agreeable, they will also help make our lives happier.

Step Five . . .

Admitted to God, to ourselves and to another human being the exact nature of our wrongs.

When we live with the fear and pain of an alcoholic situation—affected by someone else's drinking—we often feel we have so much to hide: the distortions of our lifestyle, our fears and our feelings of guilt. We pull back from encounters with people and live in a shuttered world.

In the Fifth Step we reach out to discuss with another human being what has so long been undiscussable. For many of us this is the means by which we rejoin the human race after the isolation of living for years with the pain of alcoholism.

In our isolation we had lost our sense of proportion. With our self-esteem so battered we felt our faults were too grievous, our thoughts too bad and our secret schemes to get out of the mess we were in, too ugly to confess.

When we finally admit to someone else all the dark corners within us, we usually find that the listening Al-Anon member isn't at all shocked. Bouncing our past behavior off another person cuts it down to size. The reaction often is, "So what's the big deal? I did the same thing, I felt the same way."

We are no longer alone, caged in with our unhappy guilt. Someone else knows and understands. We have a kinship with another human being and we realize that even though each one of us is unique, we are all also the same. Even more, the details of our problem are so typical.

As we talk it out, we sort out our thoughts. Saying it aloud helps us hear what we really think and the echo gives us other meanings.

Growth is an ongoing process. We find we are taking the Fifth Step when we speak up at a meeting, talk on the phone with a friend or write to *The FORUM*. Each time that we are able to admit to ourselves and to another person, we become more free.

Then when we admit to our Higher Power we see our pluses and minuses from still another perspective. From that view we can leave the pettiness behind and be more generous to ourselves. We can begin to forgive ourselves for our wrongs because now we are beginning to deal constructively with removing them and replacing them with more positive attributes.

Step Six . . .

Were entirely ready to have God remove all these defects of character.

Even after we have taken our inventory in Step Four and admitted our wrongs in Step Five, we can arrive at Step Six and still be uncertain about our defects of character.

We feel comfortable doing things the way we have done them for so long—even if they don't work. Years of rationalizing and justifying have covered our shortcomings with a veneer of righteousness. We continue in the same roles: giving loud lectures to the children—believing it's for their good; going out of our way to be helpful to friends and co-workers—to satisfy our own egos; demanding too much of ourselves; "managing" a husband or wife—just to avoid trouble.

We progress when we look deeper at ourselves and recognize that the parts we are playing are actually defects which add to our troubles. Being the heavy-handed parent, the over-helpful friend, the perfectionist, the controlling wife or husband isn't making our life any better—or helping anyone else. When we gain this insight we realize how necessary it is to change our responses.

Once we see ourselves in a new light and feel different about our place in the scheme of things, we'll be ready to have God remove our defects of character. If we're not completely willing we'll soon find out. We'll have a relapse and find ourselves right back in the old unproductive pattern.

We may butt our heads against the stone wall over and over again until we are so uncomfortable, so sick and tired of hurting, that we'll finally cut out the nonsense, recognize the reality of the situation, identify our part in it and decide once and for all that we don't want those defects that give us so much pain.

Then we'll be entirely ready to have them removed and can trust God to help us remove them. Then we'll be able to live much more easily and happily.

Step Seven . . .

Humbly asked Him to remove our shortcomings.

Those of us who first encountered this Step before our faith in a Higher Power was strong, found it a huge hurdle. How can "He" remove our shortcomings? I asked.

I battled that personal pronoun "Him" for a long time. Now, after many years of reflection and working this Step, I still believe that it can be taken symbolically. It does not necessarily mean a personal deity. It can also represent energy, divine force, ultimate good, or anything else that works for us. As Dag Hammarskjold said, "a wonder, the source of which is beyond all reason."

But even after we are comfortable with the name Him or anything else we choose, how does it actually happen, this removal of our shortcomings?

For those who have no formal religion the only thing to do is to test it—let go of our defiance and ask for help. See if by having faith in a Higher Power of our understanding we can grow, improve, reach out. It means changing our outlook. It means seeing ourselves, the people around us and our life situations with different eyes. It means not taking ourselves too seriously and being able to laugh at ourselves.

Our world changes when we look for the good, no matter how small, in every situation; when we are not ashamed to love ourselves and feel worthy, even if no one else seems to give us acclaim; when we can respond to, or at least have compassion for, other struggling, unhappy human beings.

We become allied with the forces of goodness, kindness and beauty available in the world. Then the bitter, resentful, angry feelings in us are quelled. We have, without our realizing it, allowed the positive to work in us and effect a change. We find our shortcomings are lessened and we are no longer shortchanging ourselves.

Step Eight . . .

Made a list of all persons we had harmed, and became willing to make amends to them all.

What exactly are amends? At a recent meeting a member said, "I think of two words, 'a mend,' and I consider amends the mending of relationships."

When we see the Step in that light, it becomes a lot simpler. We don't have to delve back into the problems that may have caused a rift. We don't have to remember the hurts, omissions, guilt or harsh words that caused the harms. All we have to do is be willing to start mending the break in understanding, in communication, in love, or whatever.

All mending and healing involves forgiveness. At the base of most sickness, physical, mental and emotional, is resentment. Healing can begin as soon as we let go of those resentments. We must forgive life and whatever life has done to us. We must forgive ourselves and what we have or have not done. We must find it in our hearts to forgive others, not condone what they have done, but let go of the bitterness, anger and resentment of it so it does not make us sick.

When we don't carry with us the whole heavy history of the past, we can meet as a potential friend, each person we have harmed. We can proceed as though the bridge between us is repaired, the gate can open again, the pathway is mended and we can walk forward to greet them.

Step Nine . . .

Made direct amends to such people wherever possible, except when to do so would injure them or others.

The story is told of a young father who felt sorry for having spoken harshly to his little boy so he picked him up and hugged him. But he was holding a cigarette and he burned the child. He said he was sorry and in a second contrite hug, the cigarette again brushed his son's skin necessitating another apology. The child said, "Daddy, if you're sorry, why do you keep on doing it?"

This can happen to us. With the best of intentions we may be doing injury over and over again. In trying to correct a past harm we may inflict fresh wounds requiring new amends.

Considering this, it is sometimes impossible to make *direct* amends. We may have to make *indirect* amends instead. If someone's reputation has been damaged because of our careless words, reopening the issue with apologies may do more harm than good. That's when we can only make indirect amends, by not indulging in further criticism of others and by squelching gossip whenever we find it.

If we have covered the alcoholic's bad checks, made up excuses for his absence or in other ways controlled and managed his life, trying to relive those situations or arguing them out again can't help. What we can do is let go and allow the other person to assume responsibility for his or her own life without our interference.

We may through death or separation no longer be in contact with someone we had harmed through hiding or misrepresenting the truth. Then, instead of allowing an unresolved deception to fester in us, we can make amends by being more honest and open in all our subsequent dealings.

In taking this Step, we can also apply it to ourselves. If we have courageously and honestly done all within our power to make amends, we can forgive ourselves for our past mistakes—as long as we don't keep repeating the same one.

Step Ten . . .

Continued to take personal inventory and when we were wrong promptly admitted it.

In our journey of change through the Steps we transfer our focus from the alcoholic in our life to our own self. We begin to feel more comfortable with our personality. We learn we can become fully alive and enjoy self-respect and esteem. We don't need to put ourselves down. We can celebrate the super things we have going for us.

Even though we have made progress, we will no doubt keep on doing things that cause problems for us. We can inventory those characteristics that inhibit our joyful living and try to correct them. When we find something that makes us uncomfortable, we can turn it around so it will work for us.

In doing this it doesn't help to heap guilt or remorse on our heads. We can be objectively aware of the attitudes and actions that cause us problems so we don't repeat them. If we are honest and truthful, we can be gentle with ourselves. Instead of being unduly harsh and critical, we can relax into our positive attributes. We can acknowledge it when we have done something right. By believing in and strengthening the good we are capable of, it will happen more and more often.

We can use this Step as a daily reminder. It will keep us on course and correct any potential trouble spots before they have time to build up. If the Fourth Step is the 20,000 mile service stop, this is the daily check up on gas, oil and batteries.

Step Ten helps us redress the wrongs we often inflict on ourselves. Instead of being a rod to chastise, it can become a staff on which to lean in finding faith in ourselves and greater spiritual understanding of the nature of our life.

Step Eleven . . .

Sought through prayer and meditation to improve our conscious contact with God as we understood Him, praying only for knowledge of His will for us and the power to carry that out.

So often we ask, "What is God's will?" "How can I know?" This Step tells us that prayer and meditation provide answers. If we open our minds and truly listen, we will get an indication of what is best for us.

This conscious contact with God as I understand Him can come, as it did for me during my vacation, when I was swimming in a lake in Finland by starlight after sauna, and when I was standing in an old stone church with well-worn pews where people have worshipped for hundreds of years. It also comes when I'm at an Al-Anon meeting in any part of the world and share common feelings and it can come when I'm walking down the street of my hometown.

The final portion of this Step, "the power to carry it out" was illustrated for me as I traveled on the moving sidewalks in the airport at Amsterdam while they repaired the hydraulic system of the plane for five and a half hours.

Those long conveyer belts moved steadily along. If I faced backwards and walked against the onward course, I stayed in exactly the same spot. Stuck! If I faced in the right direction and just stood still, I was carried along passively but I heard the creaking of the machinery and felt the unevenness of the motion.

When I walked forward, however, going gently but firmly with the inexorable movement, I felt as though I was flowing along, carried on cushions, effortlessly, joyously. And I thought, this is how smooth my life can be when my steps go along with God's will.

Sure enough, they repaired the plane and I arrived back home safely and serenely.

Step Twelve . . .

Having had a spiritual awakening as a result of these Steps, we tried to carry this message to others, and to practice these principles in all our affairs.

Some people see lights or hear voices, but this is certainly not necessary or even usual in a spiritual awakening. After working the Steps, we perceive that we are more than body and mind—there is a spirit within us. With this awakening we realize what we see or hear need not be heavenly visions or voices—the insights and words can come to us from members at meetings.

It is our spirit that responds to the principles of the program. Our spiritual sense recognizes beauty, a Higher Power, hope, joy and love. It is with our spiritual sense that we practice honesty, simplicity, acceptance, generosity.

How strange and wonderful it is that with this heightened awareness of the intangible qualities of life we find a very tangible strength. It works physically and mentally as well as spiritually. When we acknowledge our own spirit we find we have more energy to work and play, greater ability to face the situations in our life realistically.

We also increase our communion with other people. We are able to rise above our seeming differences and antagonisms and recognize their spirit. This lifts our communication to another plane. Instead of contention and argument, there is understanding and compassion. We also rise out of our narrow concerns to reach out a hand to help others who are suffering.

A spiritual awakening is not a great revelation we have to wait for. When we are awake to the spirit within us, it can happen in every daily encounter.

Planning or Projecting?

As THE NEW YEAR starts, we look ahead wondering what is in store for us. Plans, resolutions, anticipations are part of our thoughts. Our best resolution, however, might be not to project into the future.

It's often difficult to know if we are making sensible, necessary plans or if we're projecting. When a teenager borrows the car we can make sure he has had sufficient driver training, is insured and knows what procedure to follow in the event of a mishap and then let him go. That's planning. We can do what needs to be done in order to be ready to meet a potentially difficult situation.

But if we worry the whole time he's gone, if we upset ourselves thinking of all the possible disasters—that's projecting. We are then making an emotional response to something that might never happen. What a waste of energy!

I know I have worn myself out worrying that bills could not be paid or that my husband's being drunk would spoil his niece's wedding. Such worry immobilized and exhausted me.

There's also the trap of overplanning and trying to cover every single eventuality. When we do that we project our fears and burden ourselves with the responsibility of trying to control the outcome.

All our projections need not spring from fear or anxiety. Our energies are wasted just as much if we futilely project wishes or dreams. If we hook in with our emotions to anticipate exactly what will be, we may be setting ourselves up for a letdown. Even if what we hoped for happens, it probably won't be exactly as we had programmed it; and we won't be in the frame of mind to see and accept the good of that version. We'll be overwhelmed by our disappointments.

Self-Aware Laughter

VICTOR BORGE, THE pianist and comedian, tells the story of what should have been the lowest point in his life, his arrival in America 38 years ago with little money, less reputation and no prospects. That Christmas Eve he bought a tree. He set it down on the terrace outside his Manhattan hotel room, stepped back, and then, as he describes, "I fell! From the ninth floor!" The terrace turned out to be a fire escape, which Borge had never seen in Europe.

"I grabbed the rails, and I was hanging, and I was scared stiff—and I couldn't help laughing!"

That ability, to see ourselves and recognize the absurdity of our situation and be able to laugh at it, often makes the difference between living in despair or with joy.

In Al-Anon we talk about detachment—not being tied to the mood swings of the alcoholic. We can also learn to detach from ourselves and our emotional reactions. By stepping back (not on a ninth floor fire escape!) and looking at ourselves with detachment, we realize we don't have to take ourselves so seriously and that the situations we are in aren't as horrendous or hopeless as they seemed. Often when I speak at a meeting I suddenly hear myself being much more objective and finding the irony in my situation.

Last week Julie came to our regular Friday night Al-Anon meeting. Instead of her beautiful, long, black, silky hair she had a huge, tousled, frizzled mop of curls. We hardly recognized her, but she was the first to laugh and say, "I touched the wrong end of a toaster." She could respond with humor to remarks like, "I see you just came from a puppy palace!" She had learned to laugh at herself even while she ruefully admitted she wished she'd never gone to that hairdresser.

In all areas of our living, when we can laugh at the ridiculous and incongruous, we stop investing everything with too much importance. If we laugh at the jokes being played on us by life, we can enjoy the humor and not be wounded.

"Laugh and the world laughs with you" is true if our laughter comes from our detachment and self-awareness.

Pass It On

YESTERDAY MORNING WHEN I walked out of a large building, the man who went through the door ahead of me took an extra second to hold it open for me. I in turn reached back to hold it open for the woman who followed me.

As I heard her "thank you," which echoed mine, I noticed she had paused a fraction of a second in her stride to hold the door open for the person behind her.

That is a simple and unexpected string of courtesies in the busy, bustling city of New York. It reminded me of the children's game when one small child punches another's arm and says, "Pass it on!" And I started thinking, what am I passing on?

It's easy to feel wounded and retaliate with a sharp jab or a verbal thrust. Too often, though, we pass on the hurt to an innocent third party, possibly a child or friend, who happens to be in our path when we react.

Pass it on can also be played with words. Children in a circle whisper a phrase from one to another. What is said out loud after the original words have made the rounds is invariably unrecognizable from the first statement. When adults do this it's called gossip and the effects of passing on whispered innuendos can be viciously destructive.

Sometimes it's hard to stop and think and not pass it on, whether it's a sharp word, a mean action, or the destructive patterns we grew up with in our families. We can learn to be aware of what we are passing on and take a moment to smile, to extend a simple courtesy, to be thoughtful toward a new Al-Anon member, a child, a friend or a stranger.

Courtesy-Integrity

PENNY, FORMER CONFERENCE chairman and one of our trustees, said to me with characteristic enthusiasm, "Hildegard, you'll never get into trouble if you follow the words on the elevator doors in the lobby." How many lessons in life I miss! I had never noticed them. This building, in which the WSO has its offices here in Manhattan, has the architectural workmanship of the 20's. Each of the double, gold-metal doors of the six elevators in the lobby has a word inscribed on it. Since Penny made me aware of them I often try to apply a pair of words in the context of the Al-Anon program to help make it a good day for me.

The other day my door-words were *courtesy* and *integrity*. What a great combination! Before I came into Al-Anon I was a jellyfish. I had lost my sense of self so that I merely echoed the ideas, the pattern of living of other people. I had sunk so low in self-esteem I didn't have any opinions and didn't think I was bright enough to ever have any. I meekly nodded my head when someone else said to me, "Don't you think so?" I really wasn't sure what I thought and never ventured to protest even when I felt uneasy in acquiescing.

In Al-Anon I learned I could have opinions of my own. I could even have the right to be wrong in them. I also could recognize my true feelings and have the courage to voice them. That's when I discovered *integrity*, but I needed the second word, *courtesy,* to voice it properly.

So often there are hard things that need to be said. There are truths to be faced in a marriage, with our children, with friends, in business situations. But there are many different ways to say things. Remembering to be courteous will keep my voice from being harsh, my words cutting and my attitude self-righteous. When I combine *courtesy* and *integrity* I add a spiritual ingredient to the recognition of myself and others.

Letting Go

THE OTHER MORNING, while driving alone in the car, I passed a little white poodle who was walking along the side of the road, and a flood of unhappy memories engulfed me. It brought back the day, years ago, when I was quite new in Al-Anon and had driven home from a picnic with my husband. He was drunk, but I had given in to his insistence about driving the car himself. And then he hit and instantly killed a little white poodle who had been walking proudly and happily along the side of the road.

I commanded him to stop and let me drive back to the house to tell the family we had killed their dog. Hearing the news, the children screamed and when their father went out and picked up the small, limp body, he wept.

All the pain and anger of that moment came back to me when I passed this identical poodle and I wondered, how can I let go and not let those feelings poison my present? With frustrated rage, I sped down the highway. Then words exploded from deep within me, *"I hated it!"* Just facing and reliving the emotion I had suppressed all those years was a relief. I didn't have to scream at my husband—that wouldn't help now. But acknowledging and expressing my anger out loud did help.

When I realized I had better slow down, I poked along for several miles. Fortunately I was going slowly enough to be able to turn into a rest area with a lovely view of a lake and mountains. But I parked directly in front of a litter basket with beer bottles spilling out of it. It stood between me and the view. That irony and incongruity made me laugh ruefully, which was a further relaxation of my tension. I drove up a few feet further, changing what was possible, and then finally I could enjoy the beauty of the moment, realizing that the anguish of a puppy's death a dozen years ago need not spoil my day today. The anger is gone and, though I haven't let go completely, the pain is also less.

Deeper Truths

LAST WEEK IT seemed as though so many of my family and friends were facing unbearable problems—critical illness, crucial job losses, death of loved ones, devastating money problems aggravated by alcoholism. Each time the phone rang it brought another cry for help or comfort. And I found myself carrying a heavy burden of grief and pain for all of them.

By Thursday morning the pain I felt was almost too much. If they had been my own situations I could have done something or accepted them, but I was frustrated by what seemed the unfairness of such problems being put on people who are good, kind and gentle. Fortunately we had our regular weekly noon Al-Anon meeting in the office. The subject was personal freedom but I stated my problem with little regard for it.

When one member replied and spoke of God's will, I became angry. I couldn't accept that it was God's plan to have such suffering inflicted. As others spoke to me, mostly with "Let Go and Let God," I felt they were voicing glib platitudes, easy for them, because they weren't hurting as I was. Then it was pointed out that I could express my anger at God; I could speak out at what I perceived as injustice, but it was not up to me to judge the actions of others. I needed to recognize that I did not always know what was best. I can do nothing but accept the reality that is and try to trust that some good could come from what I saw as cruelty.

As I listened to others, who returned to the topic and spoke of their search for personal freedom through Al-Anon, I began to realize something that I have to keep relearning. So often our emotions keep us imprisoned. It is my emotional response to a situation that causes difficulties for me. I can feel compassion, but I need not be obsessed by the emotions aroused in me. My bleeding for others won't help them.

When I humbly hear the deeper truths in our Al-Anon phrases, I can find the serenity to accept.

Broader Vistas

EARLY LAST AUTUMN when I visited my daughter in Vermont we climbed Mount Hunger, 2,250 feet high. We started off through lovely thick woods of tall oaks and white birches where we could see nothing but the trail ahead of us. As it wound up the mountain and we came to lookouts, we gradually could scan the upper branches of trees we had already passed. When it seemed as though we should surely be at the top, we suddenly encountered steep rock walls we still had to surmount. Getting over them gave us a new view. Finally at the summit, we could look out over the valley—and there, a new world was spread before us with the horizon pushed even farther back.

Our perception had suddenly changed. Instead of being attracted to rich green mosses on the forest floor and sunlight filtering onto tree trunks, we saw the wide sweep of the receding mountain ranges, Lake Champlain shimmering off to the west and light clouds scudding across the sun.

Our progress in Al-Anon gives us this same opportunity to broaden our vistas of ourselves and our world. When I first came to Al-Anon I felt as though I was in a thicket that could only be hacked through with a machete. Walking up the Steps of the program I began to get some space. I could see where I was. Instead of focusing on the immediate crisis, I could take a longer look.

Even more, I could begin to see myself differently and let go of limiting beliefs about myself. Each time I applied a slogan or understood a Step at a different level, I was no longer caught in fear and self-doubt, but could move ahead more boldly. I had a higher vantage point. This is the spiritual awakening available through the Twelve Steps.

A Tibetan writer, Djwhal Kahul, has said that everything is spiritual which tends toward understanding, toward kindness, toward that which is productive of beauty and leads man on to a fuller expression of his divine potential. Each advance we make in personal insight and awareness of others is spiritual growth. We can leave the thickets of distrust and discouragement and climb up where we have new worlds at our feet and far horizons before us.

Tradition One

Our common welfare should come first; personal progress for the greatest number depends upon unity.

The strength of Al-Anon is in the individual groups where we can each go to find the help, understanding and growth we need. The Traditions give groups the means to stay simple, strong and related so that there will always be Al-Anon help available for the individual.

The First Tradition states this purpose—personal progress for the greatest number. While each individual in Al-Anon is unique and important, no one individual can distort Al-Anon's message, demand too much attention or dominate any gathering without jeopardizing the personal progress of other members.

There is unity also in our working of the program. The basic interaction of Al-Anon is the sharing of our experience, strength and hope. We do this in the groups and we also share with a wider circle of members through Conference-Approved Literature. Each individual and each group is a small part of a greater whole. Keeping the Al-Anon message undiluted, retaining the simplest yet strongest structure, keeping our eye on the primary purpose—our progress through use of Al-Anon tools—will help the most people to recover from the effects of living with the disease of alcoholism.

We will retain our unity as long as we keep our priorities straight. We are in Al-Anon because we have encountered problems of living with alcoholism. Al-Anon has a practical, workable program to teach us how to live a full life for ourselves while recognizing the legitimate needs of others.

Tradition Two

For our group purpose there is but one authority—a loving God as He may express Himself in our group conscience. Our leaders are but trusted servants; they do not govern.

Before we came to Al-Anon many of us thought we needed to assert authority. Even though we felt beaten down and defeated, we knew exactly what needed to be done to stop the disorder in our lives—someone else had to stop drinking. We became self-righteous, supercritical and authoritarian. We felt that everything was on our shoulders; we had no one else to turn to.

In Al-Anon we learn we can let go of the burden. While we still take care of our duties, we don't have to take on those that rightfully belong to someone else.

While no one in the group speaks for God, we find answers for ourselves from the group. As we hear the honesty of other members' sharing we become more honest and realistic in facing our situations. As we learn to trust the group, we become more trustworthy. As we feel the concern of the members we begin to reach out in love, becoming more lovable and more loving. When we experience these spiritual qualities demonstrated through the group members, we begin to know a force larger than ourselves. We feel we are an extension of the order, justice and love of a Higher Power and begin to act from larger motives. The paradox is, that though we no longer feel we are the authority, we find within ourselves the qualities that enable us to do what is right.

When we begin to perceive how group conscience works in the group, we can apply it to our family. We realize that listening to others, giving them respect, attempting to find a consensus of agreement, looking for the humor in a situation, seeing events in a larger perspective can work in the family setting just as well as at meetings. We can, as family members, as Al-Anon members and as service members of the fellowship, work through group conscience truly as trusted servants.

Tradition Three

The relatives of alcoholics, when gathered together for mutual aid, may call themselves an Al-Anon Family Group, provided that, as a group, they have no other affiliation. The only requirement for membership is that there be a problem of alcoholism in a relative or friend.

A problem of alcoholism in a relative or friend is the only requirement for membership in Al-Anon. That sounds so simple and yet many of us battled it for years. Maybe we didn't know about alcoholism or couldn't believe it was the cause of problems in our family, and certainly we weren't able to deal with the effects of it on our own behavior.

How fortunate that we can come to Al-Anon, attend meetings and learn the program even if we are not sure whether the problem is alcoholism; when we can only say, "I think he drinks too much."

Alcoholism has been defined as being present if drinking is causing a continuing problem in any area of a person's life: physical, emotional, social, business, marital. If we see our lives affected because of problems due to someone else's drinking, we are eligible for Al-Anon. Then we can benefit from the help available when relatives and friends gather together in an Al-Anon group.

In such a group we can find understanding and the emotional and spiritual support we need. It is because Al-Anon has no other affiliation that it can aid us. We need not be diverted by members who expound on other recovery programs; we can remind them that Al-Anon has a single purpose. We do not espouse any religious creed or practice, follow any psychological bent, or subscribe to any clinical treatment. We all live or have lived with alcoholism in our home or work situation. We share our mutual experiences within the framework of the Al-Anon program. Starting from that basic groundwork, we can each find our individual strength and growth through the mutual aid of the group.

Tradition Four

Each group should be autonomous, except in matters affecting another group or Al-Anon or AA as a whole.

In Al-Anon each group has autonomy. This means it is self-governing, no one can dictate to it except the group conscience. Implicit in this independence is the responsibility for the group to conduct itself so that it in no way injures Al-Anon as a whole.

This Tradition parallels the freedom and responsibility we can acquire in our own lives through Al-Anon. We learn to govern ourselves and not be controlled or confined by outside forces or other people, whether it is our obsession with alcoholism or any other irrational or destructive condition or person. Working the program gives us freedom, especially moral independence and self-reliance. To gain freedom means to be released from bondage and oppression. Through a change in our attitude we can throw off our subservience, our unnecessary guilts and worries, our dependencies.

Yet, if we attempt to be totally self-sufficient and self-contained we can become so separate we no longer learn and develop through contact with others. If we don't reach out, particularly to our Al-Anon friends, we lose the nurturing and the healing love of the group and deprive ourselves of the opportunity to give to others. Isolation is not the answer.

Just as groups can wither and die if they lose touch with the fundamentals of Al-Anon, the Steps and Traditions, we diminish ourselves if we don't keep close to something other than ourselves—our sponsor, our group, our Higher Power. Cutting ourselves off from the greater whole impoverishes us.

Through practicing this Tradition we can find the proper balance—both in the program and in our lives—between freedom and responsibility.

Tradition Five

Each Al-Anon Family Group has but one purpose: to help families of alcoholics. We do this by practicing the Twelve Steps of AA ourselves, by encouraging and understanding our alcoholic relatives, and by welcoming and giving comfort to families of alcoholics.

We've all heard of the jack-of-all-trades and master of none. Tradition Five saves us from his plight.

By clearly defining our single purpose, we know we are to direct our efforts to the families of alcoholics. This channeling of our energies is a limitation in one sense. We are told not to take on and try to cure all the problems of the world, whether they are other drug abuse, physical abuse, overweight, financial problems, religious concerns or whatever. Al-Anon is not a smorgasbord of self-help.

We have a program in Al-Anon that addresses itself to one problem: alcoholism, specifically as the families and friends of alcoholics are affected. We have a common bond that ties us to each other and to the group—our relationship to an alcoholic; we have suffered in common. Since Al-Anon's ideas are based on philosophy and teach individuals to help themselves with the help of their Higher Power, they can also be applied to other areas in our lives. But in Al-Anon our focus remains clearly delineated. That limitation is our strength. Our efforts will not be diluted or defected. This limitation is the basis of our unity.

Tradition Five also advises us how to carry out this purpose. We don't need to get involved with therapies, dogma, scientific theories, psychological approaches. We can very simply and directly practice the Twelve Steps, try to understand our alcoholic relatives, and give comfort to other families and friends of alcoholics.

By appreciating the bounds of our program and working intensively within them, we can hope to accomplish some good and keep our own lives manageable.

Tradition Six

Our Al-Anon Family Groups ought never endorse, finance or lend our name to any outside enterprise, lest problems of money, property and prestige divert us from our primary spiritual aim. Although a separate entity, we should always cooperate with Alcoholics Anonymous.

Tradition Six speaks of a spiritual aim. Before Al-Anon, few of us were aware that this could be the central point of our life. When we were in the throes of trying to cope with the problem of alcoholism, many of us were desperate for money or, if we did have it, we were busily accumulating material things we thought could make us happy. We also acted out roles as we thought they should be played, without recognizing our genuine needs and feelings.

Al-Anon helped us to evaluate what was important in our lives. It gave us the goal of serenity and the aim to help others who have been troubled by the problem of alcoholism in their families. We can lose that peace and joy if we should again become overly concerned with problems of money, property and prestige.

Each Al-Anon group was also founded to help members find this serenity. If the group's treasury grows too big, if meeting-hall problems loom too large, if one member or a clique becomes overbearing, the spiritual aim is lost. When the group becomes entangled or identified with any outside enterprise, no matter how worthy, the central goal of the program—to help families of alcoholics through the Al-Anon program—becomes distorted.

In our groups, as in our private lives, if we focus on our spiritual improvement—that is on intangible, desirable qualities—we will find balance.

Tradition Seven

Every group ought to be fully self-supporting, declining outside contributions.

Like all Traditions, this one developed in response to the experience of early groups in AA and Al-Anon. They found that when they accepted contributions from sources other than the members themselves, there were often strings attached, favors expected, subtle pressures exerted, and they lost a measure of their freedom. In following this Tradition, groups avoid countless complications. Self-support has made the groups, and Al-Anon as a whole, strong and independent.

In our personal lives, self-support is also essential. When we first come to Al-Anon we're too confused to know what to do, we don't trust ourselves to make decisions. We feel desperate for some strong person to lean on—often it's the drinker who disappoints us again and again.

In Al-Anon we discover personal reserves we didn't know we had. Through reading the literature, applying the Steps and sharing with other members at meetings, we begin to feel differently about ourselves. We affirm our worth, we trust our judgment and we can make decisions on our own.

The only unfailing support and lasting personal security for any of us lies in our strength within. It is the security of knowing we have the spirit and inner resources to deal with situations. It also includes contact with our Higher Power as a source of strength. With that wellspring and our own growing confidence, we have the self-support we need. We no longer need to rely on someone else to prop us up.

Tradition Eight

Al-Anon Twelfth Step work should remain forever nonprofessional, but our service centers may employ special workers.
The essence of Al-Anon is sharing. We are not a teaching or training program. There is no place for professional counseling in the meetings or for persons setting themselves up as authorities who know all the answers. The workers employed in our service centers for their special skills are trusted servants.

In Al-Anon we recognize choices and decide what answer is best for us. No one tells us what to do. Instead we find help from our fellow members who, through example, show us how to find resources within ourselves and in contact with our Higher Power.

This basic strength of Al-Anon—finding our own way—was graphically described in a recent letter from a member in Nova Scotia. She wrote, *"I'm so grateful that our program does not have professionals doing the work. I remember when I first came into Al-Anon feeling so inadequate and full of fear. When I could clear a coffee cup or pass the basket at meetings I started feeling useful. I was somebody and no one could take that away as long as I didn't allow them to. As I started growing, I was able to give some more of myself. There isn't anything more beautiful to me than seeing Al-Anon and Alateen members expressing their love for each other. It was this kind of love that helped me to begin to like myself and want to change myself."*

Changing ourselves, motivated by the love we find through the program—this is the heart of Al-Anon Twelfth Stepping. It is a special kind of caring. It is totally nonprofessional, but it works. If we added up the number of years the members of any group have dealt with the effects of the disease of alcoholism in Al-Anon, we might find there are few who could match us in actual fieldwork. We share the accumulated strength of practical knowledge.

Through Twelfth Step work we grow in the program and help other members. We are not professionals, but our loving concern is therapeutic.

Tradition Nine

Our groups, as such, ought never be organized; but we may create service boards or committees directly responsible to those they serve.

In Al-Anon, members work together for our common welfare. We do not need to be organized into a hierarchy or ranking of grades of members. We are all equal. In order to function, committees of service members can deal with specific aspects of the program, such as public information, distribution of literature, work in institutions. But in each case, the service committee is directly responsible to the group, area, assembly, or other gathering of members with whom it works.

Any potential misdirection or usurpation of control can be avoided if there is an honest examination of where responsibility lies and to whom any person or group of persons is accountable.

We can solve many difficult situations in our personal lives if we appraise them with this measure. Are we in trouble because we are assuming too much, taking on matters that rightfully belong to others? When we make all the decisions for our spouse and children we have forgotten that many times we can serve better by allowing others to have responsibility for themselves. If we have an overeager sense of duty and an overinflated view of our own importance, we'll keep running the show. An honest evaluation of our responsibility to those we should be serving can give us a better perspective.

The opposite extreme is if we shirk our obligations, copping out by blaming other people or situations. In the course of living we are responsible to family, coworkers and group members for our conduct and our share of tasks.

Finally, are we aware of our responsibility to ourselves? We cannot serve others unless we have done what is right for us, in the larger point of view.

Tradition Ten

The Al-Anon Family Groups have no opinion on outside issues; hence our name ought never be drawn into public controversy.
What hat are we wearing? What role are we playing? This Tradition helps us differentiate.

By the time we come to consider Tradition Ten we have accepted Tradition One—the unity of Al-Anon, and Tradition Five—our singleness of purpose, to help the families and friends of alcoholics. These are the points on which we can all agree. Outside issues can only deflect us from our common welfare and our sole purpose. So as Al-Anon members we do not become involved in controversy, nor take a stand on public issues.

As individuals, however, when we speak for ourselves and not for Al-Anon, we have the freedom to do whatever we choose.

Recognizing what role we are in is essential in order to understand our proper function in many areas of our lives. When we confuse our individual rights and needs, and our responsibility and loyalty as a member of any group, we can get into trouble. Wearing our individualist's hat when it's important to be a supportive member of a family, company or organization can do damage to the social group. Also, neglecting to step out of the prescribed social role of a group can stifle our individuality. There's a need for balance. The person who stays in the role of parent or spouse and doesn't ever see himself or herself as an individual is not functioning fully and freely. But the newly emancipated person who says "I'm taking care of *me"* and neglects family obligations, is also not functioning fully.

When we are aware that there is a distinction between being a group spokesman and an individual speaker, we can choose the appropriate action for us to take each situation.

Tradition Eleven

Our public relations policy is based on attraction rather than promotion; we need always maintain personal anonymity at the level of press, radio, TV and films. We need guard with special care the anonymity of all AA members.

What we *do* shouts louder than what we *say.* This is what attraction rather than promotion means. If I tell you I am serene, it has much less impact than if I act serenely. Living the Al-Anon program, reaching out to share it, are the means through which we can best offer it to others who need the help and healing of our fellowship.

Our conviction and enthusiasm is for a program through which we have found a spiritual awakening as a result of the Twelve Steps. Realizing this, it is easier to understand and practice the anonymity mentioned in this Tradition. We have the option to reveal ourselves any way we wish within the fellowship, but at the level of press, radio, films and TV, we remain anonymous. The program speaks for us and we speak for it—by example as much as words.

The principle of anonymity does not in any way restrict us in letting anyone in the community know about Al-Anon. By informing them of the availability of help through our fellowship, we may be a means of extending a lifeline. Remembering always that we are one strand in that line, one link in a chain, will help us keep our perspective in regard to our personal anonymity.

In the same way that we appreciate the cloak of anonymity available to us, we extend that reassurance to each member, newcomer and whoever comes to our group. We don't give mere lip service to the idea of anonymity—we live by the principle of being worthy of trust.

Tradition Twelve

Anonymity is the spiritual foundation of all our Traditions, ever reminding us to place principles above personalities.

Spirituality, when defined in terms of an individual, can be considered as negation of the small ego in us and an acknowledgment of the greater, God-inspired soul of each person. In this sense, anonymity, the spiritual foundation of all our Traditions, enables us to go beyond ourselves, rather than twisting and confining everything to our own narrow limits.

Our small ego is more likely to react to the people involved in a situation, while our larger self can recognize and respond to the principles in it. Someone may have a very helpful Al-Anon experience to relate, but if we judge the person talking rather than the idea being expressed, we can't benefit from the message. When we allow our anger toward a person, our fear, prejudice, or even admiration, to spill over into our response to what they are doing or saying, we are not taking an objective view. We are allowing our personal ego to backfire from someone else's actions. In our daily living, as well as in our understanding and interaction with Al-Anon, we build healthy, purposeful, workable relations when we don't get mired in personalities, but can transcend our ego and face the realities.

This ability to practice true anonymity in a spiritual sense is fundamental to Al-Anon. Doris H. from Oklahoma City writes, "If the Twelfth Tradition is turned around and we place personalities above principles, we are on our way to breaking all the Traditions." Anonymity is indeed basic to our unity, to our single purpose of helping families of alcoholics, and to the recognition of our leaders as trusted servants who do not govern.

Al-Anon is a program of personal discovery and fulfillment. The anonymity this Tradition presents is not a denial of ourselves, but a realization of our larger potential, an expression of ourselves in a wider framework, a means of reaching out to the meaningful, the everlasting.

Shaping the Future

IN THE GRANDMA MOSES museum in Bennington, Vermont, one of her sayings hangs on a sign over the table where she painted her pictures, "Life is what we make it, always has been, always will be." When I read that I realized again that Al-Anon gives me the tools to make my life. With the new year stretching ahead, it's a good time to decide what I will make of it, whether the next twelve months will be bright or gloomy. My attitude and actions can determine it. I can shape my future.

Using Al-Anon's program, I can change my attitude even if the circumstances remain the same. In people and situations there are usually both good and bad aspects. When I can see the good and build on that, I'll not only feel better, but may help the best elements to emerge.

When I sit like a blob, immersed in my personal concerns, sighing, self-engrossed, the future looms dark and threatening. But when I am open to life—stop to talk to a child playing on the sidewalk, engage in a stimulating discussion on ecology with my seatmate on the commuter train, look up to enjoy the architecture of buildings and the blue of the sky, walk along singing, even if I'm off tune—then I fashion a much happier reality.

Sometimes reality is truly bleak. It's hard to let go of the negative and see the positive when we are frightened, helpless, lost. That's when complete faith and trust are necessary to know there is a boundless reservoir of good available. Love, good fortune, even needed money can come to me when I truly trust. I can't let disappointments, bitterness and unhappiness dim the spark inside of me that keeps me in contact with a power far beyond me.

While taking responsibility for my life, I know that a higher force is available to me. By being conscious of it, that power can help carry me through the coming year—only 365 days. And I can live them only one at a time. If I use the program to shape each day as well as I can, the coming year will be a good one.

Moving On

LETTING GO OF THE PAST isn't easy. I find I can't do it all at once, I seem to have to do it in stages. But recently, with the help of Al-Anon, I made a great deal of progress in both a practical and symbolic way.

I've just moved to a new apartment. When it's necessary to sort and put all of one's belongings in boxes, pick them up and take them to a new place and then unpack them there, it's a good chance to evaluate what's worth carrying along. Books that are my friends I can't discard, even tattered paperbacks. Dishes and knickknacks are much easier to let go of. How many cake plates do I really need?

But my biggest decision came when I faced a huge box of letters accumulated through all the high school and college years of my husband's and my courtship and all those long, lonely years when he was in service overseas. I had already brought the whole collection along when I'd moved from our house. I knew I shouldn't bring it with me again in this move, but I couldn't throw those letters out without reading through them once more. It was painful at first and revived a lot of "if onlys" and "might have beens."

Yet the longer I read on, the more I realized that this was an emotional attachment that was alive mostly in my dreams. It wasn't real anymore. If I held on to it, I was clutching something that didn't exist. I couldn't live with it today, because it had no reality.

Suddenly I felt much freer. I was no longer burdened with my feelings of the past. There was a lot of good in it and I don't want to deny that. So I have kept just a few of those letters. But I won't pack them all up, or carry with me in my heart the dreams and regrets from former years, to discolor either my view of the present or my hopes for the future.

Loving Acceptance

RECENTLY MY HOME GROUP asked me to be one of the speakers at our seventh anniversary. I've been going to this Friday Night Step Group for the last six years and speaking, as always, gave me a good opportunity to reassess where I am.

I had made big changes in my life in the eight years I had attended my first home group. But what I needed when I started going to the Step Group was healing. Al-Anon, again, worked its magic. I was accepted—accepted for just being me, no matter what my shortcomings, my defects of character. That simple, nonjudgmental acceptance was what made it possible for me finally to accept myself. And when I could accept myself and get to know myself through working the Steps, then I could begin to trust in myself.

What a beautiful freedom to start feeling that trust—not to have to turn inside out to try always to please others and make sure everyone else is happy. Not to depend on the opinions and beliefs of others. I can take whatever I hear and process it through me; decide, do I buy it or not? Emotionally, too, I don't have to depend on others for my joy—grasping and aching for affection and approval. When we have learned to accept and trust ourselves, a deep reserve is available within.

Each time I speak in Al-Anon, whether it's in a small meeting or large, I draw upon that reserve—and find it strengthened at the same time. The uncritical acceptance of Al-Anon members that helped me to rediscover myself comes through—that same wonderful feeling of love, concern and support. Invariably I find that though I have searched myself to find what I can give, I instead come away having received so much more.

An Unseen Force

EARLY ONE MORNING, while there was a hushed stillness on the land and each tree stood motionless, I looked up at the sky. There, wide bands of white clouds hung suspended. The different textures of the streaks caught my interest. Some were smooth, others were rippled like sand on a beach. As I watched them I suddenly realized that the entire mass was in motion. An unseen force was driving them eastward. That force was a wind invisible to my eye, and yet with such power! All I could see of it was the effects of its power.

My life, too, has something propelling it, even though I don't feel any motion where I stand. Too often I remain unaware of it because I cannot see it—touch, taste, smell it. Yet I can make contact with that power greater than myself. And when I recognize it, I feel less buffeted and tossed about. There is also a gentleness in that force; when I learn to move with it, it cradles and protects me.

The spiritual awakening that came to me through the Al-Anon Steps shows me how to find and use that unseen force in every area of each day in my life.

Balance

WATCHING A BALLET on TV the other night, I remembered what a friend who is a dancer told me. She focuses on one point and as she twirls, she always comes back to look at the same spot. That's how she maintains her balance.

The point that keeps me in balance is Al-Anon. When I keep myself focused on the principles of the program, I don't lose my footing. When my gaze was fixed on the alcoholic and all the family problems alcoholism brought on, I was totally unstable. Only through finding a center in myself did the world stop tilting.

That center developed for me through working the Twelve Steps. They gave me a different view of my life and my functions—without guilt, fear and the other negative emotions. I perceived I could dance to my own tune and not in lockstep with someone who was unwilling to see where the steps were leading.

Each day, however, I need to reaffirm my focus. Contact with a power greater than myself gives me this axis. It is the connection which strengthens the core of me. It keeps me from spinning off on tangents—whether of being anxious and overly conscientious or too exuberant. It helps me keep the activities of each day in perspective, so that events don't loom out of proportion.

The necessity of finding a balance point implies motion; there's less need to worry about steadiness when we are stationary. We can dare to move, we don't have to stay stuck in one place, once we figure out how to keep our equilibrium.

With our eye on the higher goal, we can master the basic footwork and build it into a beautiful choreography of new knowledge and experience, knowing that our central focus will keep us poised.

As I pivot around my center, that hub of stillness and strength will maintain my balance no matter what the outward turmoil and movement.

Forgiving, Forgetting

LATELY I'VE BEEN wrestling with a phrase we often hear at meetings, "forgive and forget." It's easy to forgive injustice if we don't care deeply about the person or the cause. But when we are keenly affected and allow anger to consume us, forgiving is much more difficult and painful. That, however, is the most meaningful time to put this principle into practice.

When I invest energy and emotion in reacting to something that seems to me to be unfair, I give it power over me. What I can do instead is acknowledge the other person's uniqueness and accept his or her right to be wrong. Then I gain power over my own life and can find constructive avenues for my energy.

In Al-Anon I read I should ask forgiveness for even making a judgment of someone else. I don't know if I'll ever be able to be that objective, but I can at least realize that I am powerless to change other people. Also I need only the willingness to feel forgiving toward them one day at a time.

Concentrating on "give" in the word "forgive" helps me become less involved. I can grant space to other persons and give myself space from them. That's the emotional detachment we acquire in Al-Anon. When I stopped living through my husband's career and resenting what I saw as a waste of his artistic talent, I was able to read again, return to a full-time job and develop my own interests. Giving up the resentment made room to accept the love available to me. "It is in giving that we receive."

What do I "get" if I "forget?" Perhaps I needn't literally forget, but I can end the regretting that accompanies destructive remembering. When I let go of a situation, peace comes over me. I get the strength to act calmly and judiciously. I get the freedom to continue my life unencumbered by negative emotions.

Conscience

ON SUNDAY FOLLOWING the World Service Conference I took a long walk in the rain. The buds on the trees were just about to burst into full leaf, the air was misty gray and I had time to reflect on this year's theme—Group Conscience in Action. It had been a particularly enlightening Conference through the spontaneous expression of the group's will and I tried to figure out how abiding by group conscience strengthened the voice of conscience inside me, my aspiration to be morally good, my own "Jiminy Cricket" as that elusive ideal was symbolized in the children's story of Pinocchio. What qualities did it call forth in me?

The basic attribute is, I believe, *humility.* I must recognize that I am part of a whole. Any overinflation of that part, any pressing of myself forward, lessens my ability to recognize the conscience of the group. When I don't feel emotionally compelled to control what others say or do, I have taken a step toward humility.

The next trait is *tolerance.* If I am on the majority side of a question, I need to welcome the expression of differing opinions. They, too, have their worth. Incorporating conflicting views in a consensus often results in a strengthening of purpose.

If I am in the minority, on the unpopular side of an issue, I need *courage* to speak out when necessary. Only an informed group conscience can function effectively and I have the responsibility to let my ideas be heard. Then, after I have made them known, I must surrender to the whole, whether or not my views are taken into account. This requires wholehearted *acceptance* of the decision of the group. While I remain part of the whole, I must abide by its directives.

Accepting group conscience often calls for a tremendous *faith* that, in the long run, the good will triumph. Letting go of an issue, turning it over to a Higher Power—whether that is the group itself or a power guiding the group—demands *humility*. So I was back full circle to the first and basic characteristic that putting group conscience into action both demands and instills in my own conscience.

I touched the dripping wet twigs and the tiny, perfectly formed, pale gray-green oak leaves and felt reassured that all these qualities, if only just emerging, would be able to develop and be life sustaining.

Open Sesame

WHEN I WAS A CHILD I used to say, "Open Sesame," pretending that this mumbo jumbo would unfailingly bring about what I desired. Sometimes it seems as though I'm still waiting for some magic words to help open doors to a new and better life. That's not how it works and yet, when I change my attitude in Al-Anon, possibilities magically unfold that lead to new challenges, new serenity, new love.

I couldn't find those entries when I kept looking backward into old rooms, old ways. I defeated myself for years by freezing on the threshold to the past. I had to become willing to close the door behind me without being paralyzed by the fear that there would be nothing ahead. It takes courage to risk, to step forward, to be sure that "whenever God closes a door He opens a window."

Also, I was hampered by trying to hold ajar the gates I felt my husband should walk through. Now that I am no longer his doorman, I am free to try to find my own openings.

Progress began for me when I ventured through the doors of Al-Anon. There I saw that instead of being in a long dismal tunnel leading to nowhere, I could picture myself in a corridor with many portals of possibility. It takes faith to believe that I can choose one that will be unlocked.

When I stop knocking frantically, demanding that specific doors swing wide; when I trust that what is right will happen in due time and am willing to take what comes, not what I expected; when I prepare myself for whatever is to be, by acceptance of myself and my responsibilities; when I believe in the wisdom and justice of my Higher Power instead of bewitching commands, then "magically" barriers slide back and the way opens before me.

If I am humble and accepting enough to walk through that little door at the end of the hall instead of waiting expectantly at the main entrance that I thought I deserved, I may discover unexpected treasures.

My Space

WHEN MY TRAIN was on strike recently, I had to commute to New York by bus. One morning I realized it wasn't only the heat, rain or inconvenience that was making me arrive at the office with less than my usual bounce. I felt crushed, hemmed in. My space was being intruded upon.

The person sitting next to me on the two-hour trip was neat and clean, but I felt myself cringing against the window, trying to make myself smaller and smaller. Suddenly I recognized those feelings as the same I had had when I was backed against the wall by the alcoholism of my former husband. But now I decided I could move back and take the part of the seat that was rightfully mine. I could claim elbowroom for myself.

It isn't easy to take a stand and speak up, but Al-Anon gives me the confidence that I have the right to be myself and the courage to act on it. Fortunately, I was carrying a rather large purse and I put it across my knees so that it extended just to the line that separated the two seats. When it touched his knee, he had to move over—I had defined my area.

I am beginning to learn how to set those boundaries where I work, live, socialize or interact in any way with other people. Al-Anon's slogan Live and Let Live sums it up perfectly. I have the right to live, but I also must be aware of the rights of others. While I can define my space, I must not trespass on theirs. Overstepping into places where either one of us doesn't belong builds resentment. Being sensitive to both my needs and that of the other person, leads to harmony.

At times, however, no matter what I do, my space will be violated. Through working the Twelve Steps I build within myself a reserve core of strength and serenity. Then when I feel my space is invaded, either physically or emotionally, I can find refuge in that room within, knowing that this too shall pass and I will be able to breathe freely again.

Lilacs

LILACS HAVE ALWAYS been one of my favorite flowers. One of the things I missed most when I left my husband and our house seven years ago were the lilacs in our garden—pale blue, double white and deep mauve. Each spring I enjoyed seeing them come into bloom in the gardens of the town to which I had moved.

One morning, about two years ago, I particularly yearned to feel and smell the sweetness of wet lilacs as I drove by them, but I decided it wasn't for me to have just then and I went on to park my car and catch the train to work. And there, in the parking lot, lying on the ground in front of me, right in my path, was a small branch of purple lilacs, damp and fragrant. I felt as though God had sent them to me with the message that if I just do what I have to do, go along my path, what should come to me, will. I don't have to push or go looking for it.

If I keep hunting anxiously for what I want, I'll be setting up barriers that will prevent it from coming to me. The answer lies in developing resources within myself, making my happiness today from what is at hand, rather than searching for some elusive ideal. Then, inexplicably, when we are whole and happy in the day, the future becomes filled with remarkable surprises.

I never thought I would ever marry again. I never looked for Prince Charming, and in these seven years that I've lived alone I've found Al-Anon love in the support of my group, challenge and fulfillment in my work, joy in the beauty of music and nature. I truly felt content and thought my life was complete.

But there was so much more in store for me—John came into my life and we are to be married early next year. The name John means gift of God and I truly feel that, by letting go and letting God, the greatest joy and reward has come to me.

New Beginnings

MY LIFE, AS I ANTICIPATE my coming marriage, is on the threshold of a new dawn. While I look forward to serving as editor of *The FORUM* for many more years, there will be a new dimension in my personal life. But we are always in the process of beginning—when we start school or a new job, have children, when we come to Al-Anon, begin life in retirement or after a divorce. In fact each day is the opportunity to begin again.

Being at the first of the year heightens the sense of a fresh start and I reflected the other day on what I have learned in Al-Anon that will help me deal with changes in the future.

It has been said that the secret of happiness is being involved in something or someone else. Before Al-Anon I was involved with an alcoholic drinker and it did not bring happiness. I was "helpful Hildie," desperate for approval and interacting destructively. I am grateful to Al-Anon for giving me the tools with which to build my self-esteem, and the friends in the program who reinforced my inner confidence and strength. Without that new attitude I would not have had the courage to venture to change and become involved to mutual benefit in work and with people.

When I began to apply detachment, I found freedom to move. The essence of detachment was explained by the poet T.S. Eliot when he said we must learn to care and not to care. If we are involved in manipulating the outcome, we are bound to be defeated by life. It is in being committed and caring enough to do our utmost, and then letting go to accept whatever happens, surviving even possible defeat, that we become free. Detachment is not the absence of love, but the absence of anxiety in love.

A sense of humor, being able to laugh at myself, helps enormously to keep things in perspective. And faith is essential to muster up the courage to remain detached. Through Al-Anon I found I could trust myself. I learned to have trust in other people, even those who disappointed me at times. Above all, I found that I could trust God.

Armed with these Al-Anon tools of inner confidence, absence of anxiety, a sense of humor and trust we can look forward joyously to whatever new beginnings are ahead for us in this bright new year.

Lighthearted

"A MERRY HEART DOETH GOOD" was written centuries ago, but it's still true. In Al-Anon we find that when our hearts are merry, it brings joy to those around us but it does the most good for us.

Before Al-Anon we were weighted down with such heavy burdens, overwhelming anxieties, we could barely lift our heads each morning to go on. When we have found Al-Anon, some of that leaden load is taken off our hearts.

An essential part of our recovery is learning how to laugh. Though we can laugh at ourselves, especially when we take ourselves too seriously, laughter that's loving doesn't poke fun at other people or set them up for ridicule. In Al-Anon we begin to live with a sense of fun and excitement and even to appreciate the absurdity of so many life situations.

When we are overtired or not up to par physically, it's hard to maintain that perspective. Recently, after minor surgery, I was feeling misunderstood and put upon by some difficulties and was too frustrated to see the humor of the situation. I couldn't even get through a prayer without having my negative thoughts intrude and interrupt me. I had to rise above an oppressive feeling of resentment, stop railing against what I felt was wrong. By truly detaching and consciously making contact with God, despite my own interference, I was no longer mired in the behavior of others. When I didn't feel I had to prove I was right, I became lighthearted and free.

Joy is contagious. When we walk into a house, we can immediately sense whether it is full of that good-natured vitality—the yeast and bubbles of living. We can do so much to enliven the atmosphere and keep our homes from being flat by letting the family know they are appreciated and loved.

But the main benefactor of a happy attitude is ourselves. When we are open to see the blessings right at hand, when we stop demanding what we think we deserve and become grateful for things we have been taking for granted, then we can be light of heart. Then we are open to feel light surround us, and enter into us. Becoming lighthearted is allowing God's light to shine in us.

Waiting

HOW DIFFICULT IT is to wait. Right now, as I am writing this editorial early in December, I am waiting for my first grandchild to arrive. He/she is already a week late and I am becoming increasingly impatient.

Impatience robs us of appreciation of the present. I have wasted hours, days, months, even years waiting impatiently for what I wanted.

Certainly waiting for sobriety consumed aeons of time. By setting up my own time frame and demands I robbed myself of any possible joy in the moment and even the ability to function effectively. My concern for the future interfered drastically with my life in the present.

I often become impatient with my own growth and healing. Instead of appreciating the progress I've made, I make myself unhappy because I'm not already at some distant and maybe even unattainable goal. Working the Steps need not be a grim task if we develop compassion for ourselves. Compassion and patience share a common Latin root, pati, which means to suffer. While there is suffering in both, compassion adds the grace of sympathy—understanding in the waiting.

Even anticipation of joyful times, when we are impatient, diminishes the quality of the period in between which can have its own special happy excitement.

Waiting for time to pass, something to end, something to begin, a phone to ring, a letter to arrive, a car to pull into the drive, can reduce us to frantic motion or the complete inability to act. This is the point to redirect our nervous energy into useful activity—clean up a drawer, read a book, take a walk—anything to change our focus from the future to the present.

When lack of patience is combined with concern over the outcome it becomes much harder to wait. That's when I must remember to let the consciousness of my Higher Power's presence overcome whatever anxieties I might have. I must let go and let God and remember that no matter what I do about it, things invariably work out best in God's time.

Creating Patterns

EARLY IN THE MORNING the maple standing at the edge of the woods casts a long shadow across the meadow grass, wet with dew. Under the noonday sun, cows find coolness in the pool of shade beneath its branches. In the late afternoon its shadow lengthens again, but while the setting alters, the tree itself stays the same.

In the pattern of life there is always constancy and change. The delicate veins in the leaves are fixed for each species of tree. Yet every season presents a different aspect—uncurled new-green leaflets, a broad summer canopy or the flaming foliage of fall. Through these transformations, the unique design of the leaf stays constant. As my life pattern is reshaped, I need to reinforce my inner being so I am not threatened by the pressures of change.

Change often makes us uneasy and we desperately need to find a stable core. Living in an alcoholic environment before Al-Anon, there was no pattern, nothing to rely on. We continually tried to roll with the punches. In adjusting to an ever shifting scene, we lost ourselves and our sense of security. With Al-Anon we become able to pick our way through the uncertainties of daily living by establishing serviceable patterns.

We stop ricocheting off the walls in our thoughts and actions in response to the alcoholic's unpredictable behavior. We start to develop a simple design of order—whether it means clearing off a tabletop, planning our activities for a morning, or taking time to read something encouraging. And those who cope with the disorder of alcoholism by inflicting rigid schedules on our days, begin to loosen up. While we need routine for living, we need flexibility and spontaneity too.

Through working the Steps we learn to stand tall and sure no matter how the patterns vary around us. In knowing ourselves, we become part of the flow of life. New schedules, new settings, we realize, are like the daily course of the sun, the continuity of the seasons, the inexorable movement of the stars in the night sky. When we have inner peace, when we know we can adapt without losing our identity and move ahead while staying true to ourselves, we will be able to enjoy the infinite variety of experience.

Daring to Dare

HOW MANY OF US NEVER venture beyond the tried and familiar. Sitting home on the sofa is security, but it isn't living.

How can we get up, overcome the fear of change and go out to meet the challenge of taking a different bus, enrolling in a course at school, entering a new job? For me, it was by trusting, by using the trust I learned in Al-Anon. It isn't necessary to go to a faraway place to have a spirit of adventure. Trusting others with my true feelings was a daring risk. But in taking it I developed an inner strength and faith in my own judgment and this gave me the courage to act.

Making small moves breaks the lethargy of inaction, dilutes the fear and gets us back in touch with reality. When we begin to take small steps, we don't get backed up to the edge of the cliff, totally unprepared, with no choice but to take one huge jump. We can start moving any time at all: speak up at a meeting, make a difficult phone call, reach out to someone with a loving gesture in spite of the possibility of rejection. How difficult it is to let down our painfully constructed defenses and allow ourselves to be vulnerable. In the Al-Anon group, where we are protected, we gain the confidence to open up to others. We learn that we survive, even if we make mistakes or are wounded. They are not mortal wounds. Healing comes from trusting ourselves enough to trust others. Involved with trust is being informed, not jumping off a cliff blindfolded, yet having the valor to try even when there is an element of chance.

In Al-Anon I also learned that trust in my Higher Power frees me. I need not dread the consequences of allowing myself to be vulnerable. Since my real value comes through Him, difficulties and misunderstandings cannot diminish me.

I am everlastingly grateful to Al-Anon for helping me to heal and become whole so I can trust again and love again and have the courage to dare. As this issue of *The FORUM* goes to press I am embarking on the beautiful adventure of marriage.

Working the Program

THE OTHER NIGHT at a meeting a member asked, "What does working the program really mean?" and it set me to thinking. Is it something we do in a crisis? Is it something we look upon as an obligation? Is it something we can talk about so we are part of the group? It probably is all of these: a life preserver thrown out over a turbulent sea, a spur to move us on and a bond with others in the fellowship. But it is much more!

Working the program means making it a part of our life every day. It helps us direct our energies, use our time creatively, respond appropriately to others, and live in peace with ourselves and the God of our understanding. The slogans are practical road signs to get us through each day. The Steps show us the direction to take in our lives. The Traditions tell how to maintain our groups and the Concepts set forth ideals of service.

If I find myself mixing into something that is not my business, I can remember to Let Go and Let God. I can know my powerlessness as I learn in Step One and make amends if I did not recognize it soon enough.

I wish I could be so in tune with Al-Anon principles that I would invariably say the kind, wise word and do the just, generous deed. But that's too much to hope for. While we can keep on improving ourselves, we can't forget this program deals with response to compulsions. The slogan, Easy Does It, helps keep us from being compulsive about the program. Ours is a here-and-now program. We pick ourselves up wherever we find ourselves, dust ourselves off and proceed from there with an air of joyousness, hope and laughter. If we worry too much about self-improvement, we may miss some of the fun and beauty of the day.

Besides, we have help. Just the other day I realized why the Steps of our program are set in the precise order they are. First we hear that we are not responsible for the alcoholic, the only person we can change is ourselves. But before we take the self-inventory of the Fourth Step, we accept the Second and Third Steps. Recognizing that a power greater than ourselves is available to us, and making a decision to turn our will and lives over to God as we understand Him, gives us the basis to go on to the rest of the Steps. It is through being open to God's help, letting go of our own will, that we can be changed for the better.

To me working the program simply means that I am willing to have God work through me.

Mini-Vacations

JULY, LAZY SUMMER DAYS, vacation time. But for many this is not the month, the year (maybe not even the decade!) for a real vacation. During the years of active drinking in my first marriage, there was never a break from the erratic routine. Even now I often feel the need to get away from the tempo of living, from being engulfed by details.

So often we say, "I have no time." But when we overcome our inertia and use imagination, we can find lots of available minutes in which to exercise body, mind and spirit. Just the other day I read that there are 672 fifteen-minute periods in one week. If I used only seven of them to renew my spirit, I would still have 665 left to do all the things that seem so important to get done.

When I take a fifteen-minute break each day—or three five-minute breaks—I come back refreshed. Without the hassle or expense of plane tickets and schedules I can travel in my mind's eye: to a broad expanse of glistening white sands on which waves tumble in; or to a flat, look-out rock halfway up a mountain where I sit and see the meadows, lakes and hills spread out before me while I taste a picnic lunch of roast beef sandwiches and fresh strawberries. In a dentist's waiting room or standing in the checkout line of a supermarket, I can take an Eleventh Step. Getting out of myself to say a quick prayer or have a brief meditation smooths out the confusion of the day's events and brings me back strong and serene to carry on with my chores.

Unlimited vacation time is available to us. All we have to do is pause for a moment to make contact with the God of our understanding.

My Page

A CUSTOM AT MANY Al-Anon conventions is to ask other members to write a note in the ONE DAY AT A TIME book on their birthday—either their natal day or their first Al-Anon meeting date. The World Service Conference, at which the Delegates of the Al-Anon groups meet annually, is no exception.

In April when we were all together in New York, I repeatedly turned to "my" page and the message kept coming through to me, "And we know that all things work together for good to them that love God."

Before Al-Anon I despaired. I felt totally alone and inadequate to deal with what I saw as my unique problem—someone else's drinking. I couldn't imagine that the pain I was living through could work out positively for me in the long run.

Listening at meetings I began to feel the support of the group. And through the love of those members I could feel the love of God. With Him and my fellow members I was no longer alone. Now I can look back and appreciate the growth and understanding that came to me through overcoming the difficulties I experienced.

Meeting members from all over the world at the World Service Conference reinforces the realization of this common bond we share, and also our common goal—to help spread the life-restoring message of Al-Anon. In our fellowship, as in our families, we may not always agree on the best way of carrying out our goals; but we learn in Al-Anon that a change in our attitude is what makes the difference. When I listen to someone expressing an opposing view my reaction to it is up to me. My attitude changes if I put love of God ahead of my own pride and ego, and if I trust that others are motivated spiritually. It brings back harmony to what could have been a personality clash.

Over and over again this is demonstrated when Al-Anon

members work together lovingly. In group meetings, in committee sessions and at administrative councils, that spirit of openmindedness makes it possible for us to hear each other. And along with reasonableness, we need love—the love of God and love for each other so that we can all work together for good.

Powerful Powerlessness

STEP ONE HAS ALWAYS been the hardest Step for me. When I was in an alcoholic marriage it took me years and years to realize I was powerless over another person and finally to let go of the problem. Now in my new marriage my private life is full of happiness and contentment. In other areas of living, however, I find I must continue to apply Step One. How wonderful that Al-Anon principles apply in all our affairs!

Too often I find myself rushing in to fix, manage or make right something over which I am powerless. Then the frustration and anger such action generates makes my own life unmanageable. It's Step One all over again.

Since we've moved to an apartment in the city, I've had to change my home group. Listening there, as though hearing it for the first time, I gain new insight on powerlessness. Last week an old-time member of my new group said she was able to let go when she recognized there are circumstances, happenstances, that occur when she is no longer in there managing. When she admits the reality and no longer tries to change it, things happen. Solutions come she had never even dreamed of. She recognizes these occurrences as a power beyond herself.

Facing the reality of critical illness in someone I love, or petty bureaucracy, or injustice, inefficiency, unkindness, I must acknowledge what is and not wish vainly for the way I want it to be. I will accept people and things as they are. I will hold no residue of resentment. I cannot let negative emotions from one part of my day spill over and pollute another part. I will define what I have power over right now, this minute, and attend only to that.

The beauty of applying Al-Anon is that when I truly let go of things over which I am powerless, I discover a reservoir of power within myself. When my energy is no longer drained by futile, negative emotions, I find purpose and serenity and contact with a power far beyond me. It suffuses me with calm. That contact, that peace is powerful, joyous and productive.

Peace Within

THE OTHER NIGHT I was suddenly wide awake at 3 AM and couldn't get back to sleep. Since I was staying at a small vacation cottage, I couldn't move around, shampoo my hair, get a glass of milk or even find something inspirational to read, without waking the entire household.

As I lay in bed, and troubled thoughts, fears and remorse loomed larger than reality, I realized it was up to me to change the landscape in my head. We learn in Al-Anon that changed attitudes can improve the situation. How could I quiet my racing thoughts?

Quiet was the key word. There was plenty of it outside. The waves barely lapped the shore and the peepers had long since been silenced. But I longed for silence, peace within me.

Just saying those words to myself—quiet, silence, peace—helped. I found I was taking long, deep breaths; my hands unclenched. As I kept saying them and feeling the tranquility of the night come into me, those frantic thoughts faded gradually; there were more empty spaces between them. That left room for me to get beyond the worrisome cares and put them into perspective. I was able to say a simple prayer and really feel it. Suddenly I was calmer, less fearful and angry. When a worry intruded again, I just reached back to those feelings of calm, I breathed deeply, relaxed and let the anxieties dim.

When I'm mentally frantic, I feel like a record with the needle stuck in one groove from which there is no exit. That's certainly how my life was in an alcoholic marriage before Al-Anon. In this fellowship I learned that there are always alternatives—I didn't have to stay stuck in the same mental rut. By calming anxieties within, changing my emotions and attitudes, I can reach out beyond myself and recognize other ways that are constructive. Peaceful relaxation brings on not only healing sleep at night, but opportunities for living throughout the day.

And His Brother

AT HOLIDAY TIME WE hear a lot about the brotherhood of man and goodwill to all. How much do we really make these ideas part of our lives?

Last summer, on an island off the coast of New England, I had a lesson in what they mean. One morning I called to my husband, "The garbage men are coming." "No," he answered quietly, "it's Jesse and his brother coming to get our trash." Suddenly, instead of faceless, nameless nobodies, they became real to me even though I had never met them. By giving each person dignity as an individual, instead of lumping people into groups, we can more easily recognize them as our brothers.

It may be easier to keep that one-to-one response on a small island, where everybody knows each other. Yet how often, in the isolated island of an alcoholic home, I reacted to the alcoholic not as an individual but by self-righteously criticizing him as being "like all alcoholics." It is such generalized judgments of groups which keep us from accepting people as people.

We must be able to accept ourselves before we can accept others. At my first Al-Anon meeting, I felt the genuine nonjudgmental acceptance of me as an individual. It changed my perception so I could eventually accept myself without self-condemnation. That led me to be able to see others as individuals, to separate them from a crowd and acknowledge their distinctiveness. Even more, through discriminating, I could decide what I liked and what I didn't; what behavior I considered acceptable and what I need not accept. I didn't make a judgment, I made a choice.

When we get beyond the collective, faceless mask of a group and identify the individuals, each becomes a person and not an object. There is the excitement of discovery and the joy of identification. There is acceptance of somebody's singularity instead of a compulsion to mold the personality into a preconceived form.

Sometimes it is the most difficult to accept uniqueness in someone close because our own idea of what he or she should be shuts our eyes to what is real. Accepting the real and the best of somebody is a form of love.

Recently, Margaret N. of New Zealand wrote in a letter to *The FORUM* that in Greek there are four words for love. The one that met her need to understand her relationship with her family was "agape"—defined as unconquerable goodwill and the determination to see the other person's highest good.

The extension of this love from the deep feelings we have for our immediate family is the birth of universal brotherhood. We go beyond our family and even our fellowship and sense the uniqueness of spirit and the divine spark in all individuals. Then we feel unconquerable goodwill to all our brothers.

Vanquishing Fear

THE BEGINNING OF THE new year is a time to look back—and look ahead as well. Yet looking ahead can be risky. If we had anticipated twelve months ago all the happenings of this past year, we would have been overwhelmed. Somehow, taking them one day at a time, we managed to survive the valleys, enjoy the peaks and arrive at the beginning of a new year.

The year before us may also bring unexpected changes. It would be so nice to have everything neat, tidy and predictable. One of the most difficult aspects of living close to the disease of alcoholism is that feeling of being on uncertain ground, shifting sands. When we don't know what to expect, we imagine the worst will happen. Projecting our anxieties casts long black shadows of fear before us and dooms us to walk in shade, not sunshine.

Change is inevitable and anxiety is normal, but there are creative ways to adapt to change and the Al-Anon program shows us how.

Changes, even happy ones, require readjustment. In this past year I have been called upon to play many wonderful new roles of wife, stepmother, grandmother. Through Al-Anon I become increasingly aware of the person I am so I can fill each new role with my true self. I no longer need to turn myself inside out to please everyone else—which ends up pleasing no one.

Since the anticipation of change often creates the greatest distress, the one-day-at-a-time idea helps me most. Instead of looking ahead with dread of the unknown, I can build on the core of strength inside me to live through today. That act of courage makes me stronger, braver, so I change.

We are all different in some way from what we were a year ago. By thoughtfully applying Al-Anon to my life, I may even have become more mature instead of only older. I may have learned from the experiences of the past day or the past year—both good and bad.

Too often, fear makes me see changes as a personal threat. Perhaps, however, I can find the positive features in each change to defuse the fear. And accepting an inevitable change graciously can be a means of growth for me.

Most of all, I can face the future with less fear when I continue to improve contact with my Higher Power and trust that the changes I need to face can be for the better, even though they are painful now. I will vanquish my fear and creatively adapt to change through that trust.

Vulnerable to Love

AFTER MONTHS AND YEARS of living with hurt, I didn't want any more of it. I walled off the pain. Much as I wanted to feel close to someone, I didn't dare reveal my deepest feelings for fear of another reaction, another time that giving of myself would be used against me. While I maintained my defenses, I couldn't truly love.

Within the protection of the group meeting, I took the chance of opening up, of becoming vulnerable. The nonjudgmental acceptance of me there assured me I was in a safety zone and could venture to uncover some of my real emotions. When they were accepted and not trampled on, I no longer needed to pretend. I could start to tear down the facade behind which I had been hiding. Then I could take a good look at who I really was.

Being accepted lovingly in Al-Anon and learning to deal with myself honestly, I discovered strengths I never knew I had. Instead of cowering in fear behind deep-seated barricades of self-deception, I gradually found inner reserves. When, through applying the Al-Anon Steps, that person inside of me emerged with thoughts, feelings and conviction, I found that being open and vulnerable wasn't so dangerous anymore.

There's always a hazard in trusting and we don't want to leave ourselves wide open to those who are untrustworthy—I was hurt and disappointed many times when I did. But it no longer crushes me.

I learned too that depending on others for their judgment of me makes me too vulnerable. I don't have to take the opinions of others as my measure of myself. One time a few years ago, when I felt a deep rejection from someone I cared for, I could see I was still the same person I had been when I had been told I was wonderful. I hadn't changed from great to awful in the meantime. The other person's idea of me had changed and I did not have to take that. I can listen, but I do not have to accept any distorted perception. I trust my own judgment on whether it is accurate. I don't have to remain stuck with feelings of anger, dread and self-pity.

The breach in the wall does more than let our fears out. There is also a passageway for love to come in. First of all comes God's love. When we begin to trust a power greater than ourselves, even if it is only through the Al-Anon group at first, then we feel love entering in to heal us and make us strong.

For a long time I denied I was still holding back, staying numb behind hedges of distrust and anxiety. It takes much longer than we expect to erase the memory of hurts. But slowly we can grow and reach out, realizing we don't need fragile shells of protective masonry around our hearts if we have an inner core of vitality. Accepting the risk of being vulnerable can reward us with the opportunity for unbelievable bonuses in reciprocated trust and love.

Taking Note

RECENTLY, IN THE BACK of a bookcase, I came across an old notebook. Looking through it brought back all the heartache of the years of living with an alcoholic, for I had used it as a diary through a twelve-day vacation.

That had been a rare opportunity to get away from everyday cares and I had tried to apply one Step in succession for each of the vacation days. I used the questions in THE DILEMMA OF THE ALCOHOLIC MARRIAGE as a guide and wrote down in that little pad the questions on the Step that seemed to apply to me. Then I rated myself with a plus or minus for all the incidents of the day and how I had responded to them. I had managed not to make a sharp remark when I found bottles packed in my rainboots, but I "opened my big mouth" and lectured him on several other occasions.

I came to the realization that my own thinking had to be straightened out. I had to be less self-conscious and more conscious of being myself. I learned to live for just the one day and at the end of the vacation I felt as though I had truly had a spiritual awakening and achieved a closer contact with God.

My life has changed so much in the dozen or so years since then. I have remarried—and that was a gift from God. John is not qualified to be a member of either fellowship, but through my years of continued attendance at meetings and his generosity of spirit, the Al-Anon principles are very much part of our lives. Genuine caring, respecting the individuality of each other, acceptance, laughter and spiritual goals are just naturally woven into the fabric of our marriage.

It's easy when the other person lives by Al-Anon. But what can be done when in everyday working relationships other people seem to demonstrate the opposite qualities? Even then, and especially then, Al-Anon principles are our best defense. Instead of running through my mind all the things I should have said, or could have said, or will say next time, I must muster up tolerance, compassion, love and acceptance. That little notebook did more for me than recall the past. It brings right into the present the work I still need to do on the Steps to bring the sanity and serenity I seek. But I need not forget that I have come a good way along the journey of discovery. I can take note of where I am and, building on the lessons already learned, I can proceed.

Selfless Help

THE FOUNTAIN OF YOUTH and health may be closer than we imagine.

The other day I came across a simple statement that read: "Formula for retaining health—find something to do which involves helping others. Then keep doing it. And don't try to be what you are not." This basic wisdom sounded to me like Al-Anon's theme, pass along understanding.

I came to my first meeting with an ulcer, having swallowed resentment and anger for so long. In those early meetings I began to understand I could improve my situation, regain my health. I could do something about my own life. Al-Anon is a self-help program.

The help I needed to help myself was the love and sharing of experience offered by other members. I heard how they applied the Twelve Steps to deal with alcoholic situations in their home. That showed me how to apply the Steps to my life.

The next phase of healing is sharing with others how we put into practice the principles of Al-Anon. Coming to meetings and listening to another troubled member is a way of being helpful. Through words, and especially example, we can help others who have had the same heartaches.

Service in Al-Anon is a further enlargement of helping others. Bringing the cookies and coffee for the group, taking responsibility for chairing a meeting, means going beyond ourselves for others. I remember the good feeling I had when I was first asked to be the secretary of our group. I felt accepted, trusted and I welcomed the need to keep going to every meeting.

We are fortunate to have the privilege of carrying the message of Al-Anon to those who need its help and comfort. A genuine smile, a word of support and a commitment to service can help others. In giving help, we help ourselves. The best self-help is selfless help.

The final recommendation of the simple formula for health also contains much Al-Anon thinking: "Don't try to be what you are not." This points out the virtue of humility—to be genuine, unpretentious, not proud or arrogant. No one can speak for Al-Anon; we speak only for ourselves and share only what is our own experience. We don't tell anyone else what to do. The principles of Al-Anon are the means of helping others, not personalities.

That old ulcer of mine healed long ago, but it's still a good barometer for me. If ever I feel a twinge, it's a warning that I'm not practicing the principles and have to straighten out my thinking. When I keep involved in helping others and being true to myself I have the key to health, serenity and longevity.

Erasing Old Tapes

THE OTHER DAY AN Al-Anon member came to a meeting very upset because he had had to take his wife to the emergency room of the hospital the night before. Even though she was not drinking now, it brought back all the other times of being in hospital emergency rooms. His present distress came from playing those old tapes.

So often we do that to ourselves. It is very painful. Yet perhaps replaying those old tapes, with new Al-Anon awareness, is the best way of reducing their tyranny over us.

That's exactly what worked for me two years ago. My husband and I were dating then and he had planned to pick me up for dinner at 6 o'clock. At 4:30 he phoned to say that traffic out of the city was heavy and he might be delayed, but he'd get here as soon as he could. From about 5:30 on I kept glancing at the clock every few minutes. By 6 o'clock I was pacing the floor, feeling that panic in the pit of my stomach. By quarter after six I was a nervous wreck. All the old tapes of waiting for my first husband, who was an alcoholic, to come home for dinner were playing in my head. I felt the old fears, anger and apprehension.

Then I sat myself down and told myself this was ridiculous. Hadn't I been in Al-Anon long enough to know I could live in the present moment? Why didn't I recognize the reality of the current situation and see it was very different from the past? This time it need not play out to the disaster I expected. I was dealing with a different person, in different circumstances. But even if that weren't changed, I was different. I was no longer the compulsive over reactor.

When I took an Al-Anon look at myself and set reality up in front of me, those bad feelings disappeared. I could put on some good music and calmly read a magazine until the doorbell rang. One old tape had been erased and was ready for a much more serene imprint.

Start Again

A COMMON SAYING in the fellowship is that we never graduate from Al-Anon. Last spring, while I was attending the graduation exercises of my youngest stepdaughter my mind wandered during the graduation address.

As I watched the lovely scene before me, I started relating the encouraging phrases of the speaker to Al-Anon. I was thinking that another word for graduation is commencement. New dawns are constantly available to me was the message I had heard in the fellowship. I never want to lose that realization of the opportunity to start again.

I can have a new beginning each time I attend a meeting, read a piece of Conference-Approved Literature, use an Al-Anon principle. As I apply the tools of the program, I can enter upon a new stage of understanding in a personal relationship or a difficult situation. When I do, serenity grows within and the circumstances surrounding me seem to improve.

Someone recently said of a beloved member, "His duty, as he saw it, was to make himself a stone in a foundation on which others can build with confidence. It is a better world because of his efforts. What a wonderful world this would be if we were all like him."

The graduation speaker tried to inspire his young listeners with such spiritual dedication. It is an integral part of our slogan, "Let it begin with me." Each one of us can face each new day with the resolve to apply just one principle of the Steps—humility, honesty, courage, generosity, or whatever moral quality could best help in that particular situation. We can begin to be the person we would like to be.

We too, just as if we were young graduates, even though we never graduate from Al-Anon, have the opportunity to commence our life anew each day, eagerly and enthusiastically, knowing we can make a difference.

Protecting Myself From Anger

RECENTLY A READER WROTE to take issue with the idea of "righteous anger" which he had read, in one of Al-Anon's books. He saw it as "a dangerous and serious threat to our recovery."

His letter arrived at a good time for me. It reminded me that, even though I may be "right," I cannot afford the luxury of being righteously angry because of what that consuming emotion does to me.

Anger is insidious, unless we can acknowledge and defuse it. For years, even while living in an alcoholic marriage, I denied I was angry and so all the negativity I didn't admit revealed itself in tremendous fatigue and the physical illness of ulcers. When I came to Al-Anon I learned, very gradually, how to recognize my true emotions and, even more, deal with them so they didn't harm me or anyone else. Yet they can still cause me problems.

There's a lot of energy used up in the emotion of feeling wronged while being "right." If I become obsessed with that resentment, all my energy is wasted and I lose the opportunity to correct what may possibly be a "wrongly" handled situation.

I must keep working at separating the emotion of anger from the mental exercise of deciding what is "right." It is only with detachment—and even love for the person I see as "wrong"—that I have any hope of being objective, dispassionate and kind enough to have any influence for good in the outcome.

The feeling of anger isn't right or wrong. What I let it do to me is what matters. The three qualities of the Serenity Prayer can help me protect myself.

Acceptance (without any smoldering resentment) of what I can't change can get me through the irritating hassles of tie-ups in the check-out line or even the major problems that someone else's actions cause.

Courage (from clear-headed thinking and trust in my Higher

Power) to change the things I can, can help me to speak up or act when issues of principle are involved that concern me deeply.

Wisdom to know the difference will be available to me if I don't become blinded with self-righteous rage and if I prayerfully turn for guidance to the God of my understanding.

Changing Moods

THE INFINITE MOODS of the sea intrigued me on my vacation last summer—the brooding fury of an approaching storm, the tumultuous excitement of crashing surf the next day, the joyful glimmer of sunlight on rolling waves and the muted calm of fog-flattened waters. I could enjoy each, but I did not need to make that mood mine.

Before Al-Anon, living in an alcoholic marriage, I took on the mood of everyone around me. Hearing about loving detachment in meetings helped me know I need not take other people's emotions into myself. When I stopped bouncing off others' feelings, I recognized with surprise I had feelings of my own. I could be happy, angry, sad or serene because of how I felt, regardless of the emotions or actions of others, even those of people I loved. In fact, I could be a lot more loving when I didn't just echo or react to them.

My life is much more manageable as I recognize and live with my own emotions. Yet there are times when it seems even harder, because I can no longer blame anyone else when I feel down. What can I do at those times?

The basic slogans of Al-Anon are the tools to change my mood. Just for Today keeps me from projecting gloom and doom into forever and helps me get through the immediate present without anxiety. Live and Let Live directs me to my own affairs so I don't worry about what doesn't really concern me.

Let Go and Let God takes much of the burden of cares from me because I get to a spiritual sense. Looking at the star-filled sky on that quiet vacation island off the coast of New England, far from city lights, I could easily sense a closeness with the God of my understanding.

Coming back to the city bustle and the anxieties of workaday life, however, I had some of those down feelings. Then, on my way to work, across my path in quick succession came a cheerful young blind man who made his way aboard the bus with a white cane, a man with a Seeing Eye dog confidently crossing the street, a woman in a wheel chair graciously accepting help up the curb from a passerby, a homeless woman carrying all her possessions in a shopping bag and talking vacantly to herself.

I realized with a burst of gratitude that I have eyes, I have legs and I have friends I can always talk to in Al-Anon. With a prayerful attitude of gratitude I no longer felt down. I was again in touch with that spiritual sense and remembered anew that I have the power to change my moods.

Courage to Keep On

INEVITABLY THERE WILL BE times when we become discouraged—when we can maintain no meaningful communication; when we are frustrated in getting things done; when we feel low and it is difficult to keep contact with our Higher Power. At a moment like that, I looked at the word "discouragement" and saw that at the heart of it was "courage." What is needed is the courage to keep on keeping on.

I can regain a spirit of trust in the rightness of things, optimism that it's worth the struggle, through the example of Al-Anon members and their demonstration of the resilience of the human spirit. Hearing the experiences of others who have had discouragement, and much worse, helps me gain perspective on my situation. I can learn to recognize a problem as existing in only one compartment of my life and refuse to allow it to intrude on and contaminate the rest. I can rejoice in all the good and joy that is available to me, if I don't become obsessed with one problem.

Yoko, a member from California, has been such an inspiration to me recently. She sent *The FORUM* a Sen-ba zuru which, she explained, is a traditional Japanese form of prayer. It is one thousand cranes delicately fashioned in the ancient art of origami (Japanese paper folding) suspended in streamers from a circle. Yoko wrote that she made these multicolored paper birds over a period of six months, in the hours when she was so desperately lonely, while her partner suffered from the disease of alcoholism.

While she was isolated and alone in the mountains, far from any meetings or members, she used her time constructively to meditate and construct a thing of beauty. Even more—she had no money, but she took advantage of what was at hand, the paper of dog and cat food bags, to create a lovely and lasting symbol of spiritual strength and hope.

In Al-Anon we also have the ability to take the most basic and practical tools, available to us in this program, to enrich our lives and the lives around us, if we only have the courage to keep on keeping on.

Special Magic

THERE IS A SPECIAL MAGIC when Al-Anon members come together. I have felt it from one end of this continent to the other—in the historic, rolling farmland of Delaware and more recently in the stark, beautiful, desert state of Arizona, site of the November Regional Service Seminar. In rooms holding hundreds of members, I could feel the love generated among people who had never met before that day. There was a common bond of caring and sharing.

What is this special ingredient that brings out the best in each one of us, that welds us together? Can we sustain those sparks of enthusiasm and inspiration, the warm inner glow of contentment? Does the outpouring of good feeling come across in all our everyday encounters? It isn't always easy, but the principles of the Al-Anon program point the way.

Love is the answer—a love based on principles, common goals, respect for ourselves, respect for one another and trust in our Higher Power's love for us.

Sometimes it is easier to love in the abstract—mankind, the poor and suffering of the world, desperate newcomers to our program. When I get to specific individuals, with all their frailties and their interaction with me with all my frailties, love is more of a challenge. I am not able to love completely until I have healed my own wounds, am faithful to my real self and am a whole person. I must be happy with myself or I cannot find happiness with someone else. Before Al-Anon I did not know my own mind or how to set the boundaries of unacceptable behavior. I am learning this now—not in the spirit of judging someone else, but with understanding of what I feel I can live with comfortably, and with recognition and respect for my own integrity.

Above all, I need an inner spiritual peace, constantly rein-forced through daily contact with the source of serenity and integrity, the God of my understanding—my refuge and my strength.

When I come to these meeting rooms where Al-Anon members gather—whether it is five hundred or five—I feel an acceptance and love of me as a person. I have the opportunity to speak out the deepest feelings of my heart and know they will be heard with caring and trust. That is the healing love that enables me to accept myself and grow strong enough to be able to give a nondemanding, nonjudgmental, principled and joyous love in return.

Friendship

JUST THIS MORNING as we were preparing this issue for the printer, including the feature on bereavement, I received news of the unexpected death of a young, yet long-time friend of mine in Al-Anon. When I visited her last week she was ill, but I didn't realize critically so. We had shared together, at weekly meetings and also social times, so many experiences of living in an alcoholic situation and growing toward serenity in the fellowship.

Through the shock of her loss I have become much more sensitively attuned to the sorrow of the members who are sharing on these pages. But Helen would, I know, want me to heed the words of comfort and hope they impart for she generously put the concerns of her friends before her own.

Today, also, a memorial service was held for the sister of another Al-Anon friend. As I sat in the house of worship and reflected on both of these events I realized how Al-Anon principles can help us to live so that when a friend we love goes, we will have fewer regrets for things not said, kindnesses not done.

I resolved to live each moment to the fullest with whatever person I am with. To listen with a totally open and loving heart. To accept without judgment or impatience the time I spend with someone. To be wherever I am at that very moment, not planning where I will be, go or what I will say even the next moment. Not to put off the note, the phone call, the thoughtful gesture that can make all the difference in my giving completely and fully in the best kind of friendship.

The time we have is fleeting at best. We are allotted but one day at a time. It is only by putting all of myself into whatever I do that I can experience the greatest happiness which is that joyful attunement of myself with another good friend.

Twin Pillars

BEFORE AL-ANON I WAS bound to the twin pillars of Want of Control and Want of Approval. My life was unmanageable because I wanted to control my first husband's drinking and yet have his approval. I didn't know all my frustration and anger were built into those pillars and that I could free myself from bondage only through applying the Twelve Steps.

Last week during discussion at a meeting, I realized anew that in any situation it is through First-Step surrender to things I cannot change that I can let go of wanting to control. No matter how misguided I may believe other people's actions and attitudes to be, I cannot control them.

How can I accept my powerlessness, give up control, without feeling helpless and defenseless? I must see I am not giving up any control. I can't give up something I never had. If I'm not in control, who is? Humility helps me recognize a Higher Power.

Yet at the same time that I try to manage, while I defy, nag and berate others for what I judge as wrong, deep inside I still want their approval of me. I am influenced in what I say or do by the desperate desire to please them. In doing this I turn over the one thing over which I have control—myself.

Each time I have a negative feeling of frustration, anger or fear, I can try to identify whether it is chaining me to the pillar of Want of Control or the pillar of Want of Approval. When I recognize it for what it truly is, I am better able to handle that bad feeling and loosen some of those bonds. I'll see I don't have control over many things. My struggle to take control over what isn't mine is what wears me out. When I see I am suffering from a lack of approval or from desire for approval I can, with conviction and self-confidence, change my attitude and actions and be less tied to people-pleasing.

It has been said that we should love our enemies and bless those who persecute us. Perhaps that means that each time someone's action causes me to have a negative feeling, I should look upon it as an opportunity to chip away at the links that chain me to those pillars. When they are gone I will float free through life.

Worlds Within Worlds

THERE ARE SO MANY WORLDS to keep discovering. I've just come back from a vacation in the Bahamas where I explored the totally new, to me, underwater world of scuba diving. Yet even in that alien environment, the admonitions I heard were those of Al-Anon.

"Think" was the most important rule of all. When the footing was gone from under me in an alcoholic marriage, Al-Anon showed me how to think, not panic. It provided the Twelve Steps to save my sanity. When I foolishly jumped into choppy seas without my air supply in my mouth, I couldn't panic and inhale gulps of sea water. I had to stop and think how to locate and then breathe through that lifesaving air hose.

"Easy Does It" was vital too. When I clutched desperately at the program and tried to go too fast, I wore myself out and got nowhere. If I frantically fought the waves and currents I used up that air supply too quickly, as well as my energy. I had to learn to trust my natural buoyancy, slowly and smoothly kick with the flippers, calm down and breathe easily.

Without "Live and Let Live," I would not have developed the adventurous spirit and confidence to embark on this venture. Even more, it made me aware of the worth of all living creatures. Having been in the marine kingdom and seen the freedom and grace of its inhabitants, I have a new respect for all who dwell there and couldn't possibly hurt any of them.

Another point of view was also revealing. As a novice in

the underwater world I was dazzled by the long white corridors of sand at the bottom of the ocean and majestic stands of elkhorn coral. My eyes caught the largest and most colorful fish. Experienced divers, however, look for rare and tiny specimens of fish and coral.

Those of us who are novices in life, no matter what our age, often make the same mistake. We see the bold and obvious but miss the small, rare insights. Think, don't panic, Easy Does It, Live and Let Live help me appreciate the opportunities for moments of joy, beauty and wonder.

I need not go far afield to find the spectacular. Close at home, when I explore my own self and my own life, I can find countless small wonders and joys. With openness of heart and mind and awareness of the delicate beauty in all of God's creation, I'll discover worlds within worlds.

As the poet William Blake wrote,
"To see a World in a Grain of Sand
and a Heaven in a Wild Flower.
To hold Infinity in the palm of your hand
and Eternity in an hour."

Detaching With Love

"NO MATTER HOW CLOSE are the ties of love and concern that bind me to my family and friends, I must always remember that I am an individual free to be myself and live my own life in serenity and joy." (ONE DAY AT A TIME IN AL-ANON, September 25th)

This is the essence of the Al-Anon concept of detachment. When I acknowledge both my love and my individuality, personal freedom is mine for the taking.

I can take it even in a most restrictive environment if my attitude is one of personal dignity, compassion for others and acceptance that I cannot change anyone else. But I can change myself. A continuing, searching and fearless moral inventory will show me when I am willful, people pleasing, arrogant or spineless.

Those qualities are destructive and confining. I must become free within myself before I can recognize the reality of my situation and the options available to me. Free within myself means looking for the greater good and willingness to surrender my will to a Higher Power. It means being able to live, love and laugh freely and joyously, finding the best in every day and every circumstance and concentrating on that.

Sometimes, however, there is the most painful decision to be made that unacceptable behavior can no longer be accepted and a more drastic change must be made. This was the difficult route I had to take when I terminated my first marriage.

I could never be free, however, no matter how far away I moved from the person or situation, if I still harbored bitterness, anger and blame. When I still held those negative feelings, I remained tied to the past and unable to recognize the new paths open to me. I had to be free within myself and reach out with love, even to those who had hurt me, in order to live serenely and at peace.

I must believe that whenever a door closes behind, a new one opens ahead. How many times I have slammed doors shut in total frustration and anger. Then I was blinded to my part in the problem and unable to open the next door. To lead somewhere good it must be opened with a loving heart.

Love is always the key. When I detach with love and close the door firmly, yet gently, I will not harbor that poison of bitterness within me. Then I will be able to unlock the next portal and find fulfilling ways to give and receive ever deeper dimensions of love.

Fran H.

Editor 1983–1987

"One of the first books I read, about a week after coming into Al-Anon, was FORUM FAVORITES. It spoke to me, a nervous, worried newcomer, in a way that was calm, reassuring and blessedly humorous from time to time. This book was what led me to seek out *The FORUM* magazine each month."

Our Shining Gifts

IF YOU HAVE DAUGHTERS, you have probably been through this scene more than once. My teenage daughter, size 10, was trying on her two bathing suits. I was sitting in the living room reading and not paying much attention to what was going on in front of the full-length mirror. Gradually I became aware of her sighs, her occasional soft moan, the headshakes at her own image. She is perfectly trim and fit and looks the way we would all like to look at the beach.

"What's the matter?" I finally asked, feeling some comment was wanted.

"Everything! It's hopeless. I look awful."

I contributed soothing noises for awhile and thought I had managed to assure her she would not be barred from the public beaches, that she looked just fine. After making what I thought sufficient allowances for a teenager's insecurities I heard the self-criticism and complaints continue. Finally out of patience I said, "When are you going to learn to look in the mirror and say, 'Thank you, God,' and really take joy in the gifts He has given you?"

This refusal to see the good in ourselves—how it persists! Even with years in Al-Anon, it is difficult for many of us to feel joyous about ourselves. Is it the toll that living with alcoholism takes on our self-esteem? Is it the criticism, sometimes almost constant, that the drinker uses to defuse his own misery and guilt? Is it a trait that gentler souls are born with, an intrinsic part of certain temperaments?

Whatever the answer, it seems to me that many of us in Al-Anon are especially vulnerable people. I love to tell newcomers, "Tell yourself everyday, I'm number one." Their eyes fly open wide and they look astonished. It is obviously the first time some of them have ever entertained even the possibility of such an idea. It is at that point I may finally get a smile from people who entered the meeting frightened and confused.

That is why a recognition of our *inner* qualities, the good in our *inner* selves, is so important. We must become aware of the shining gifts of compassion, strength and humor in ourselves. Only when we accept these gifts as an intrinsic part of our nature can we generously share them with those around us, our family, our friends, our groups. We must take time out to say to ourselves and others, "Good job—well done!" and "Hooray for you!"

Holding Up The Sky

"DON'T PUSH THE RIVER—JUST let it flow." When I heard that bit of wisdom recently I had to laugh. How ridiculous to push a river, a force of nature! And yet that is just what I had been trying to do in my own life. After my husband's death, I had been making arrangements, getting affairs settled, hurrying, hurrying, not taking the time to realize fully that there are occasions when it is appropriate for decisions to be shared, when others should be consulted, when family matters are just that—*family* matters.

The result was that I was exhausted and my children felt left out, unable to tell me how they felt. Fortunately, before any plans had been completed, my youngest child blurted out, "Why didn't you ask *me*?" Youngest children are expert at straightening out their parent's thinking!

It dawned on me then. Yes, you're right. It isn't all up to me. We who have lived with the problem of alcoholism get so used to making the decisions, to getting things done by ourselves that it is very hard to change. Ask for help? Never! Perhaps a little of our martyr role comes in there, unconscious though it may be. We do everything ourselves, saving other people trouble. We have a need to view ourselves as independent and strong. It costs a lot to let go of that image, to join the human race, to become vulnerable, needy.

And many of us in Al-Anon are worriers. Granted, there is a lot to worry about in the alcoholic situation; but some of us frequently carry our fears over into problems having nothing to do with alcohol. This perpetual expectation that the sky will fall can ruin the quality of life for ourselves and those around us. We certainly miss a lot of joy that way. I made a determined effort to cure that defect when I read somewhere, "Worry is an exaggerated sense of our own responsibility."

I have learned that when I worry excessively I am denying my Higher Power's loving concern for me. I am running on ego. I must step aside and be quiet and let the healing of the program and the fellowship work in me. Above all, I must get myself out of the way and give my Higher Power room to accomplish what He wishes in my world and my relationships.

I must stop pushing the river and *just let it flow.*

Healing Begins

SOMETIMES THE WORLD catches up with me and overwhelms me. My vision of my life and my destination, my purpose, becomes clouded. Why? Too much rush and hurry? Jet lag from the holidays? Too many people in a small apartment? The relentlessness of daily commuting?

I know when that faltering begins it's time to step aside, be quiet, wait. The peace will return, the blessed uncurling of nerve ends, the gentle release of taut muscles, the slowing of time. I must reach for the spiritual reading of the program. Admitting broader thoughts into my consciousness will lift me away from the everyday to the eternal, to peace and God.

Whether it be the frustrations and disappointments common to *all* lives or the particularly baffling ones we experience in living with the problem of alcoholism, I must turn to the

program with complete trust as I did in bereavement. Healing
begins when I . . .
> forgive others and myself,
> take time to meditate,
> focus on myself,
> deepen my faith,
> stay open to my Higher Power,
> listen for guidance.

In February the earth is on the brink of spring. Grass will
come up a tender new green, trees will leaf out and blossom
again. This miracle occurs every year and we stand in awe
and worship. Yet how much more intricately are we human
beings designed than the green wonders of the earth. We have
the capacity to renew ourselves *daily,* to rise after crushing
blows and to find life good again.

About Love

LOVE—IS THERE ANY SUBJECT in the world that has been written,
talked, sung and rapped about more than love? We all think
wistfully, from time to time, how fulfilling it must be to be
taken care of, pampered and loved.

As a wife and mother, I found joy in a simple caring phrase
from my husband or one of my children. It let me know they
understood and loved me when I least expected it but needed
it most. I'm sure the same is true of husbands and fathers.
Though some people do not show emotions easily, they too
feel the love expressed in a warm smile or gentle caress. The
security of being loved by a spouse or children is enviable.

I can remember long ago resenting the flowers and the
beautiful card my husband brought home on anniversaries. I
would think, why doesn't he give me what I really want—a
sober husband? I didn't know then that he had a disease, a

compulsion that he could not handle. I would have been kinder. Looking back I am sure he was doing the best he could.

When my daughter was a teenager I used to enjoy sitting opposite her boyfriend in the living room and calling out, "Jack's here." My daughter would emerge from the bedroom, hair shining, showered and leggy in the mini-dress of the sixties. Jack's sixteen-year-old face would light up. He might as well have had a neon sign across his forehead saying, "Wow, girl!" She would give him a self-possessed "Hi, let's go," and they would take off. I realized he was simply happy to be with her. I thought how great that he is able to love so freely. Perhaps that is even more important than *being loved*. The saddest human beings in the world must be the ones who are unable to love.

We learn the value of true self-love from one another in our groups. Once sure of ourselves, we are freer to give generously to others.

In Al-Anon our thoughts of love extend beyond marriage and family. A friend of mine told me, "In the program I learned how to love, really love other people. They don't have to be related to me."

The crowning gift of Al-Anon for many of us is the love of our Higher Power. A letter from an Alateen member who had finally found this love in his program touched me with its simplicity. He said, "God is a big part of my life now and I love Him dearly."

New Beginnings

SPRING IS THE TIME for beginning again, for discarding old ways that don't work. Shed them like a worn-out winter coat too threadbare to be serviceable. It's also the time to climb up and out of our rut and have a look around in the sunshine.

New energy is available—physical, mental and spiritual, that we can use to shake our lives up. We have choices. We have awareness. Small changes can give us the momentum that will carry us to bigger ones.

I knew two sisters once who cleaned each other's attics each spring. It was much simpler than doing their own because there was more detachment. Each knew the other's limitations— "No, Grace, you'll never get around to shortening those skirts and slips. They've been here two years now. Pack them up and out." Or, "That's not a good color for you, Helen—out with it!"

In a way we perform that function for one another in Al-Anon. "Your situation has been difficult, I know, but maybe it's time to accept, to move on." Or, "Let's see if you can do something positive to clear up that resentment. Have you tried talking to that person, writing a letter, being honest without hostility?"

We give one another courage to make good decisions. We help one another move ahead out of the shade and into the sunshine.

A Memorable Summer

THE WINTER HAD ITS share of storms, the spring its ravaging floods. Now we can turn to a softer season with hope.

We all can experience a joyful summer. I don't mean a time when everything in our lives goes right. If I wait for that condition in order to be happy, my life will be on hold indefinitely. No, I mean that you and I have to make a resolve that this summer we will seek out and enjoy what an all-loving Higher Power has given us—our pretty green planet, the ocean, the sunshine, paintings, books, parks, music, the smiles of our loved ones, the warmth of our meetings. All the things that add color and texture to our days, that fill us up; pleasures like these that enrich our spirit are especially important to us who have been affected by a loved one's alcoholism.

The saying, "A life that has not been examined has not been lived" is certainly true. If we did not examine our lives we would never learn—we would make the same mistakes over and over. Such a life would be aimless and without direction. We in Al-Anon are fortunate in this respect. All we need to do is turn to our Steps for guidance. Step Four offers us the opportunity to examine ourselves without fear. We know that we will be able to improve our attitudes and our lives by living our program.

I also feel that in another way a life that has not been *enjoyed* has not been lived. If we look deep inside with the help of our program and if we work at it, we will find that pain will pass or we will cope with it, that gusto and joy can be renewed.

Opportunities

I REMEMBER IT WAS A morning of brilliant sunshine. I walked along holding my husband's arm and my little son's hand. My compulsion, the compulsion to make him stop drinking, was in full operation. (It was many years before I was to hear of Al-Anon.) I was talking hard at my spouse, determined to open his eyes with my irrefutable logic and common sense. I was at the state where I still hoped against hope to hear him answer me, "You're right, dear, absolutely right. I'll never touch another drop."

Finally it penetrated my consciousness that we were drawing curious stares from passersby. I looked down at my two-year-old. He was wreathed in cigar smoke, happily puffing away on a soggy butt he must have scooped up from the pavement just as it was discarded. After a stomach-wrenching thought about the germs in that soggy butt, I managed to pry him loose from it. Of course he was indignant and it took a little diplomatic negotiating to calm him down. Then I had to have a good laugh about how ridiculous we must have looked sauntering along with our baby smoking a cigar!

Now, having grown considerably in the Al-Anon program, I see this incident from many years ago with new vision. The message is still loud, clear and important. Detach! Only then can I get a perspective on my life and problems. While I am spinning around in the vortex created by the alcoholic, I am incapable of running my own life and taking care of my family. Preoccupation with the alcoholic, I see now, results in the family's doing without the loving attention of the sober parent that it needs to flourish. Faced with the loss of one parent's supervision through the disease of alcoholism, how will little ones survive the loss of the other parent's care?

Why couldn't I have simply accepted my husband's company that morning as that of another adult? Why always treat the alcoholic as the erring child? Who knows how much more good I might have done for him and myself had I been able to take that one hour to share our lives with no reference to drinking.

My Higher Power strews my path with opportunities for laughter and sharing. I must be alive to them and make the most of them.

Help Break the Cycle

". . . youngsters come to feel invisible, unloved and rejected by parents whose attention focuses on drinking." (Children of Alcoholics Foundation, Inc.)

I can remember running home from school at 3 o'clock, through the streets of Manhattan, heart pounding, tearing up three flights of stairs and crashing through the door of our apartment. As soon as I saw my mother, I stopped my headlong rush, gazed at her while panting for breath. She would generally scold me for running and go on shelling peas, peeling potatoes or ironing the boys' shirts.

Never once did I say, *"I was running to make sure you were still alive, Mom."* I had a desperate fear that my mother would be killed, such was the hostility and violence generated in our household from time to time by an alcoholic father. My mother had no idea of the terrors that beset me. I kept my fears to myself. I kept my questions to myself. Everyone around me, my older brothers and sisters seemed to accept the loud voices at three in the morning, the physical abuse, the tension and hostility. So I followed their lead. I tried to be grown-up, to do the same as they did, to be quiet, to blot it out of my consciousness. Looking back, I guess I thought, *this is how it is—put up with it like everyone else.*

I remember puzzling over my father's behavior. He could be funny, generous, attractive. Hours later he would be an inexplicable monster. I think the conclusion I reached without realizing it was that he was insane. Perhaps for me, at five years of age, that was a reasonably serviceable definition of alcoholism—intermittent insanity.

I remember thinking desperately, if I were prettier or smarter or could make my father laugh, that maybe then the longed-for magic would take hold and we would become an ordinary happy family. How much easier it might have been for me and my mother if she had had the program of Al-Anon in those long-ago days. She would possibly have recognized my unspoken pain and talked to me quietly about the disease of alcoholism and encouraged me to get my fears out in the open. That is all in the past, however, and we must deal with today.

Because we have been fortunate enough to learn and grow through the Twelve Steps there is a sounder emotional future ahead today for children of alcoholics. We can share ourselves with them; help them free themselves and get ready to go joyously about the challenge of finding their talents, developing their potential, of living their own lives to the fullest.

The fears, the emotional malnutrition that may have been our lot need not be our children's or grandchildren's inheritance. We know how to do it with love and caring—let's break the cycle.

New Places, New Faces

I AM JUST BACK FROM five days in Utah. The air was crisp and cool, the sunshine bright—enough to lift this New Yorker's spirits high as a kite. The Al-Anon members I met were loving and caring, working hard to carry the message. Their welcome gave me an even greater lift.

My happy visit made me reflect on the many years I spent in despair. I knew no better. But since Al-Anon I have made a decision to pack in as much joy as possible. We all live as though we are going to be here forever; we may spend precious hours in unhappiness and sulking over what we wish we could have or do. Or we can make a resolution now to stop wasting time and draining our emotions.

One of the tragedies of living with alcoholism is boredom. Even if we go from crisis to crisis, nerves straining, that pattern in itself is eventually boring and makes us feel life is empty. The problems seem never to come to an end.

Al-Anon tells us to turn the focus from the alcoholic to ourselves. If we do that we can, no matter our age, start learning about us, start growing, enjoying, trying on our different selves, daring to be foolish from time to time, allowing the child in us out to play, the adult in us to relax and accept. Even if we go just across town to another meeting to supplement our home group, we will be finding new places and new faces that can change the tempo of our lives, enhance the way we see ourselves and help us tap deeper into the joy of life.

Happy Holidays

ENJOYMENT HAS ALWAYS seemed to me a most important part of life. For some of us this is a spontaneous, natural outgoing flow of feelings as taken for granted as breathing. People who truly enjoy life enhance the lives of all around them. That is part of the charm of the very young—a few clothespins or a big spoon and an old pot to bang on are entrancing toys to them and we laugh to see their delight; happiness is catching.

Living with alcoholism can dim the spirits of the most hardy. Perhaps this is a good time to check our joy in living, to remind ourselves that we have choices. Have we fallen into the habit of chronic worry, chronic sadness, fear and foreboding? Without even realizing it? Are we dimming the natural joy of our children? If we are working our program we can change our attitude. I can remember saying over and over, "No one in the family is in jail. No one is in the hospital. Thank you, God!"

It is up to us to set the tone of the holidays in our home, to resist the push for buying *things* that the media puts on every year. We must take time to discuss the spiritual meaning of the holidays with our children, to help them see how empty life would be with only material things, and how full life is if love and caring are there. I can remember my mother describing to the seven of us gathered around the kitchen table, how some rich children spent the holidays at boarding school or at home alone in the care of servants. I remember that my heart would swell with pity for them and I would feel content that my life was full and rich.

For twenty-four hours, we can resolve to make our children feel loved; to join in their happiness; to make people feel welcome, to turn to our Higher Power in trust many times in the course of the day to keep our love and joy radiating to all around us. If we keep ourselves constantly in His presence we will wind up each day with a feeling of satisfaction that we made it as happy as possible. We will close our eyes at the end of the day giving thanks for a serene and happy holiday.

Index of Subjects

You will find this listing of the subjects covered in our book a big help, both in planning meetings and for your personal needs.